SIT UP SUSTAINABLE SEATING STORIES

ISBN 978-0-9557129-0-6

Copyright © 2007 [re]design

Published by [re]design

1 Summit Way
Crystal Palace
London SE19 2PU
England

www.redesigndesign.org

All rights reserved. No part of this book may be reproduced in any form without written permission from the publisher.

SIT UP...

Are you sitting comfortably? And sustainably?

SIT UP gets to the bottom of sixteen seats that combine the fundamentals of seating design – user comfort, quality and style – with a passion for sustainability. The results are truly 'good' and gorgeous.

SIT UP investigates their journeys from inspiration and development into production and use. Together these tales give a picture of sustainable design practice in the UK with relevance far beyond the field of seating design, proving that design can be responsible and friendly to people and the environment. SIT UP aims to entice, inform, and motivate designers, manufacturers, specifiers, retailers, purchasers – and everyone who sits – to make more sustainable choices.

The SIT UP designers range from new graduates to long established companies. Each has a unique take on sustainability, with their own distinctive working processes. The approaches you'll find here include:

- Awareness of material choices: sustainably grown natural materials, reclaimed wood and cardboard, salvaged furniture, and innovative recycled plastics.

- Redesigning manufacturing processes and supply chains: local sourcing and selling, energy-efficiency, and user as maker.

- Considering the relationship between product and user: adaptable seats that change with the owner over time, participative design, and designs that encourage sustainable habits.

- Long-term thinking: products that last a lifetime with minimal maintenance, design for easy upgrading, disassembly and recycling.

The outcomes are incredibly varied, but all are propelled by the belief that design can help create a better world.

We hope that SIT UP will inspire the next generation of friendly seating and get more bums on sustainable seats.

So pull up a pew and discover the stories behind the seats.

SIXTEEN SUSTAINABLE SEATS

6

ALT CHAIR
AARON MOORE

12

BOURKE'S LUCK
RYAN FRANK

18

C10 SPRINGBACK CHAIR
DAVID COLWELL DESIGN

24

COCOCHAIR
ALESSANDRO ZAMPIERI DESIGN

54

ONCE A DOOR
CLAIRE HEATHER-DANTHOIS

60

POLY-MORPH
LOU ROTA

66
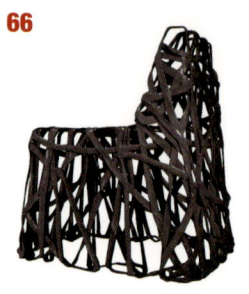
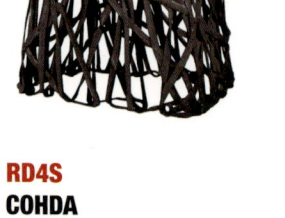
RD4S
COHDA

72

REEE® CHAIR
PLI DESIGN

30

GROWNUP STOOL
CHRISTOPHER CATTLE

36

I B POP
BLUE MARMALADE

42

JOY
ORANGEBOX

48

MAX
REESTORE

78

ROCKY THE ROCKING SHEEP
SAM MURAT

84

TEDDY BAG
ANDREW MILLAR

90

TETRIS
WEMAKE

96

YOUR STOOL 2
RYUICHI TABU

ALT CHAIR

AARON MOORE

An elegantly simple chair made from recycled coffee cups and locally grown, steam-bent ash.

Dimensions: H 700mm x W 450mm x D 450mm

Materials: Recycled plastic, ash, natural oil finish, screws

Tools: Circular saw, planer/thicknesser, mortising machine, bandsaw, spindle moulder, plane, chisels, spokeshave squares, large home-made oven, clamps, steam box, former and straps for steam bending, router templates, hand router and bearing cutters, sash clamps, G clamps

[re]strategies: [re]cycle [re]make [re]source

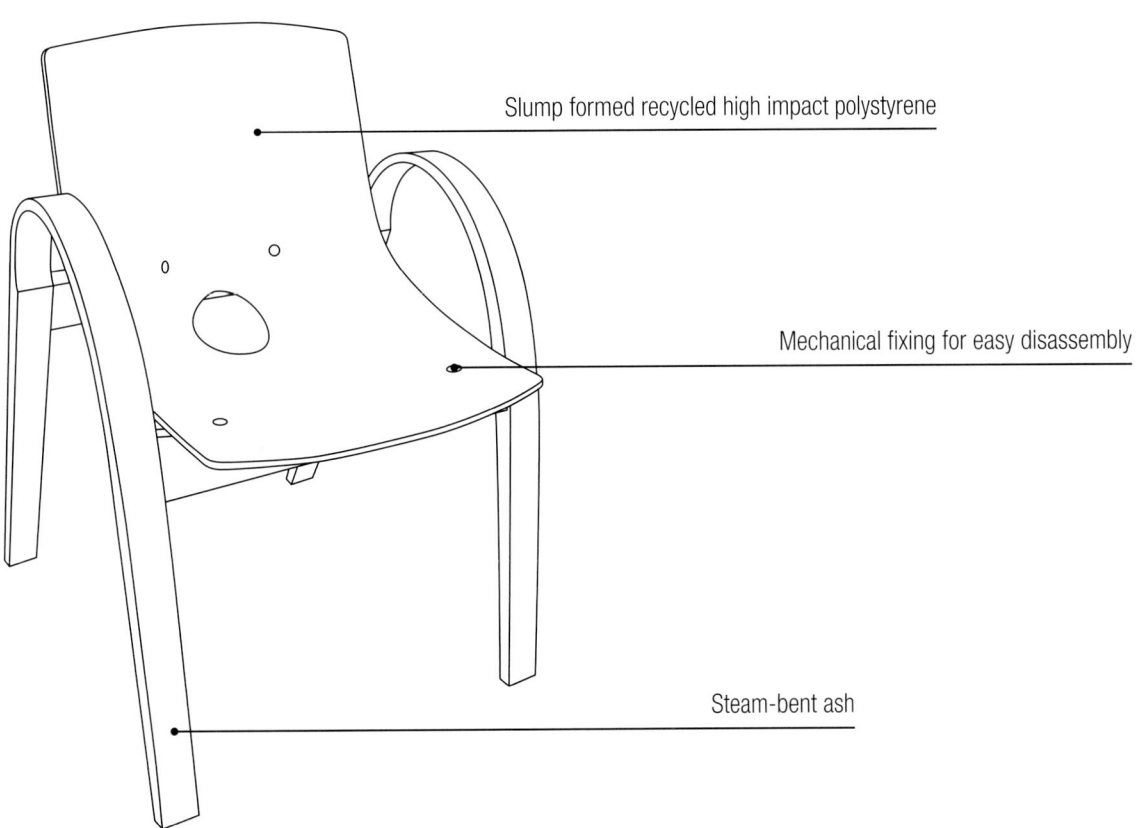

Slump formed recycled high impact polystyrene

Mechanical fixing for easy disassembly

Steam-bent ash

THE MAKING OF ALT CHAIR

[1]

[2]

[3]

The latest in a series of chairs developed by Aaron Moore utilising recycled plastic sheet produced by Smile Plastics, the Alt Chair's charcoal-coloured seat is made from used coffee cups. Having lived and worked in Africa for many years, "experiencing at first hand how precious and valuable resources are for the majority of the people on this planet", Aaron feels strongly about communicating environmental issues through the materials he uses.

Simple and energy efficient to manufacture, using minimal components and low tech equipment, the Alt Chair is intended for local production and supply. Aaron is also developing the concept of "open design" to allow others to manufacture his designs where the materials and market are available, by purchasing either CNC files, or tooling and templates.

Wood is sourced from a local supplier only 15 miles from Aaron's workshop. Their small mobile sawmills extract timber with minimal disturbance to the surroundings, and use solar powered kilns to season the timber.

[4]

[5]

[6]

The legs are made from fast-grown green ash using a steam-bending technique, which seasons the wood at the same time as forming it and is much more energy efficient than kiln drying. After being machined to shape, the legs are placed in the **steam box [1]** for about 45 minutes until malleable. They are **strapped and clamped [2]** onto the former until bent, then cooled and dried before being **hand planed [3]** and sanded smooth.

The rest of the chair frame is machined from solar powered kiln-dried ash. The whole frame is finished in natural oils.

The one piece seat/back, made from recycled high impact polystyrene, is moulded by placing a blank over a **former [4]** and **heating it to 120°C [5]**, when it slumps to take the shape of the **mould [6]**. After cooling it is simply screwed to the frame. At the end of the chair's life the plastic can be recycled again, the fixings can be reused and the timber will biodegrade.

IN CONVERSATION WITH AARON MOORE

What sparked the idea for this piece?
The need to sit comfortably with a guilt free conscience.

What is the message behind your work?
Good design does not need to cost the earth.

Do you see this design developing further? If so, how?
Yes, I think there is scope for a nuclear family of similar chairs.

What are the environmental implications of your work?
My aim is to use materials and processes that are as sustainable as possible.

Does your work have an impact on a social level?
I hope it helps to motivate people to recycle their waste.

What made you start thinking about sustainability?
My experience working in Africa where every resource is valuable and recycling is a way of life.

What makes a truly sustainable product?
Natural materials, renewable energy and a spark of genius.

How can we turn manufacturers and specifiers on to sustainability?
Eco designers have got to come up with some really exciting stuff.

…and other designers?
Scare the shit out of them.

Do you have any words of wisdom for new designers?
Don't give up.

Where do you get your best ideas?
I don't know. They seem to creep up on me when I'm not looking.

What motivates and inspires you?
My children.

What was the last object you threw away?
A computer.

What was the last thing you fixed?
A computer.

What is your guilty pleasure or biggest eco sin?
3D software that runs on Microsoft Windows.

If you could get everyone to do one thing every day, what would it be?
Breathe deeply.

BOURKE'S LUCK

RYAN FRANK

A resourceful chair built from redundant office furniture. Its curved lower platform provides storage space for magazines, books and cushions.

Dimensions: H 750mm x W 400mm x D 580mm

Materials: Redundant office furniture, FSC birch ply

Tools: CNC machine

[re]strategies: [re]claim

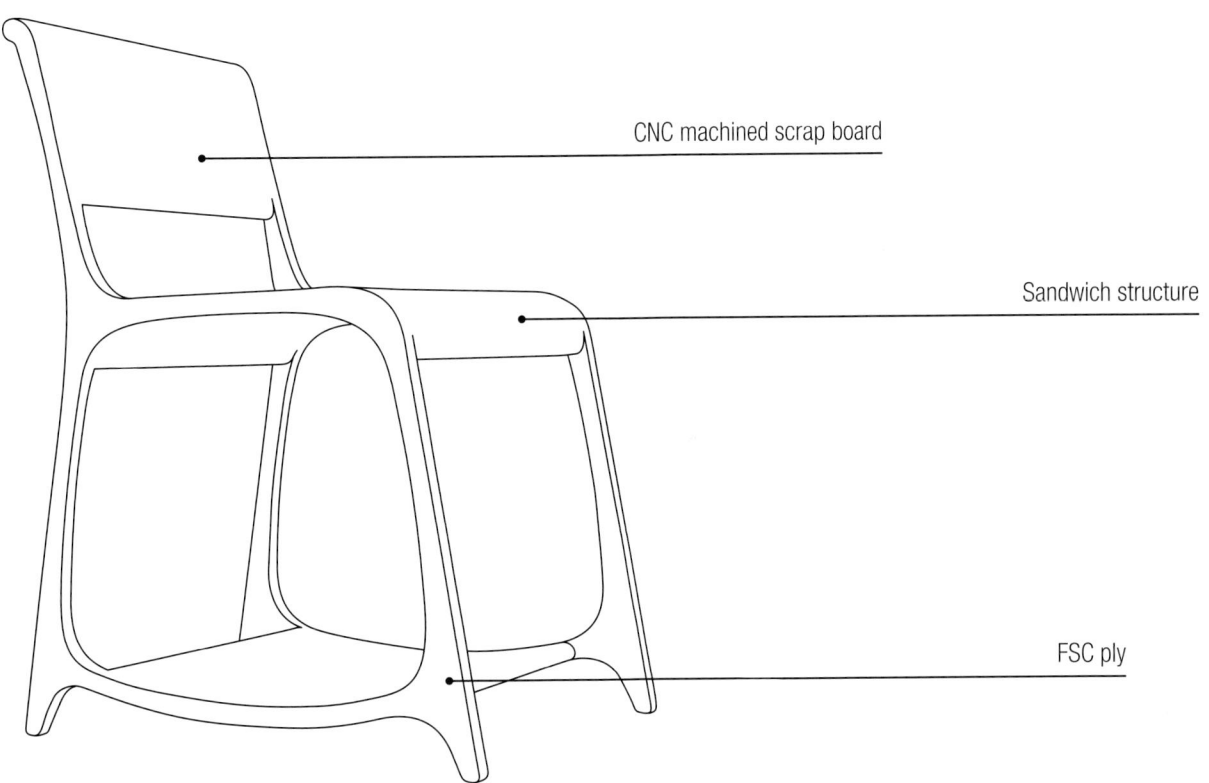

THE MAKING OF BOURKE'S LUCK

[1]

[2]

[3]

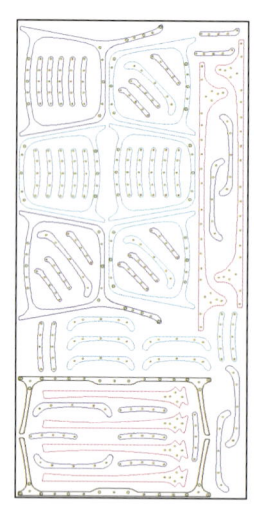

Inspired by the large amounts of sheet timber of all different types being **thrown out [1]** every week from his shared workshop, Ryan Frank started collecting them, and soon had plenty.

A few weeks before the 2007 Milan Furniture Fair, wanting another quick, simple product, Ryan designed a piece using the scrap wood he had collected. This became the first prototype that would lead to the development of Bourke's Luck. After seeing it in Milan, Portuguese company IMADEtrading approached Ryan with a request for a whole range of furniture made using the same technique.

To develop the range, a more substantial source of scrap wood was needed. [re]design put Ryan in touch with **GreenWorks [2]**, a charity and social enterprise which reclaims timber from redundant office furniture collected around the UK.

"They are absolutely brilliant," Ryan enthuses. "I went to visit them in their massive warehouse in West London... they have tons of old office desks,

[4]

[5]

[6]

[7]

shelving, filing cabinets, chairs." Some of the furniture is fixed and re-sold, some recycled and some re-manufactured – which is where Ryan comes in.

Working from **drawings of his designs** [3], Greenworks digitally cut out all the components straight from **reclaimed sheet materials** [4]. This **mix of components** [5] goes back to Ryan to be **sandwiched together** [6], creating a unique piece of furniture every time, with pieces **layered in random order** [7].

"It's a fantastic resource," says Ryan. "Each individual reclaimed component comes with a story – I love the fact that I am able to build a new piece of furniture which already has a history of its own."

IN CONVERSATION WITH RYAN FRANK

What sparked the idea for this piece?
Overflowing skips of wood being thrown out.

What is the message behind your work?
I guess there is a subtle message... don't throw so much stuff away!!!

Do you see this design developing further? If so, how?
Yes... a collection is currently in the process of going into production with a Portuguese furniture manufacturer.

What are the environmental implications of your work?
Too soon to tell about implications, but I would be happy to create some awareness.

Does your work have an impact on a social level?
Dunno, I will have to socialise a bit more to find out.

What made you start thinking about sustainability?
Just came naturally... no great defining moment...

What makes a truly sustainable product?
Besides nature, a product that can be recycled indefinitely using little or no energy.

How can we turn manufacturers and specifiers on to sustainability?
A demand needs to be created, which stems from the mainstream consumer... retailers will respond to this call, which in turn will entice designers and manufacturers to start embracing an eco ethos... I guess this takes time.

...and other designers?
Public opinion.

Do you have any words of wisdom for new designers?
Stay new.

Where do you get your best ideas?
In the shower.

What motivates and inspires you?
Festivals, they provide everything a human desires to be free, happy and inspired... music, friends, nature, camping, sun and smiles.

What was the last object you threw away?
A black sock, there are only so many holes a sock can have.

What was the last thing you fixed?
A solar powered sound system on pram wheels.

What is your guilty pleasure or biggest eco sin?
Flying regularly to Spain to go rock climbing… btw is there anyone working on developing eco-aviation?

If you could get everyone to do one thing every day, what would it be?
Send me £10.

C10 SPRINGBACK CHAIR

DAVID COLWELL DESIGN

Perfect for long conversations around the dining table, this comfortable chair is made from native, fast-grown ash. The chair's efficient structure is good-looking, flexible and supportive.

Dimensions: H 950mm x W 500mm x D 510mm

Materials: Steam-bent ash, stainless steel, organic oil finish

Tools: Straps and moulds, setting jigs, steam boxes, steam generator, curing kiln, bending press, planer, bandsaw, table saw, sanding machine, drillpress, spindle moulder, cross cut saw

[re]strategies: [re]duce [re]source

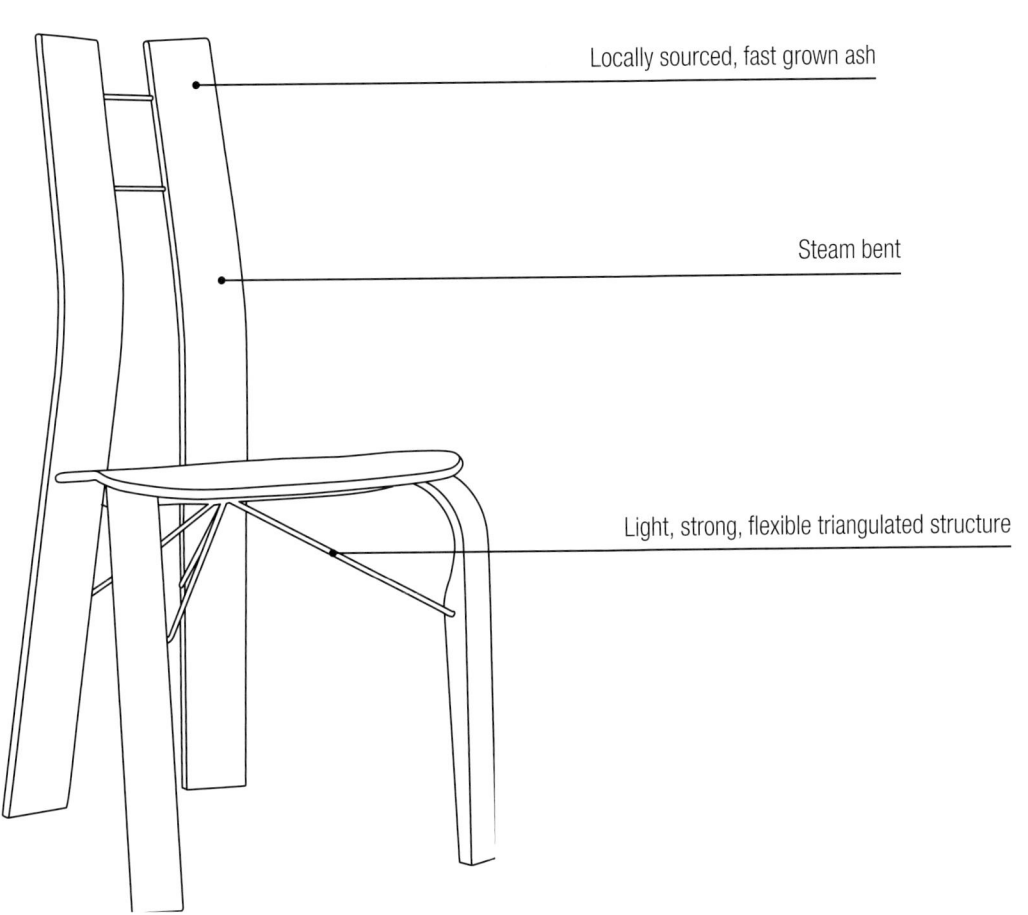

THE MAKING OF C10 SPRINGBACK CHAIR

[1]

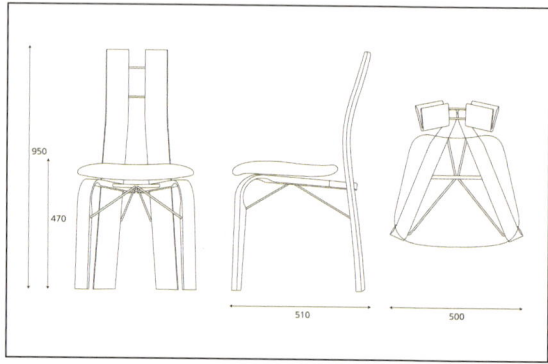

[2]

For the past 29 years, David Colwell has been pioneering sustainable design and clean production – "on the principle that an interesting answer is most likely to come from an interesting question." Traditional techniques are used as building blocks for innovation, with a focus on quality and comfort. Materials and production techniques have been selected for minimum adverse environmental impact, and to develop an enduring aesthetic that symbolizes sustainability.

David aims to make his tables and chairs "a delight to own, because they satisfy – practically and visually – and don't let you down". His furniture has an elegant geometry based on strong triangulated structures incorporating curves to allow flexibility.

The C10 Springback Chair is a **development of the original C10 [1]**, his most popular design. It is steam bent from just four pieces of **fast grown ash [2]**, joined by a light stainless steel spider which completes the triangulated structure. The new more yielding frame design makes it both stronger and lighter.

[3]

[4]

Seat options include pressed solid ash, or upholstered.

Ash is a durable hardwood which makes best use of the UK's climate and soil conditions, and is even stronger when fast-grown. Wood for the C10 is sourced from thinnings (young trees that are cleared to allow light to reach other trees, and which normally go to waste), which gives a further income to foresters.

Ash (along with Douglas Fir) absorbs more atmospheric carbons than any other timber. Ash has no sapwood, making for less waste in its conversion to plank.

Steam bending [3] seasons the wood as it is bent, using a fraction of the energy required in conventional kiln drying. David describes the process as "very efficient and enjoyable but not foolproof, making it a very good use of a **craftsman's time [4]**". Like other formable materials, steam bent timber can reduce production costs, increase strength and free the imagination to create new shapes.

IN CONVERSATION WITH DAVID COLWELL

What sparked the idea for this piece?
This is the latest in a long series of steam-bent ash chairs. This one pushes flexible structure to give more comfort and strength with less material.

What is the message behind your work?
That sustainable design can be inspirational and sexy.

Do you see this design developing further? If so, how?
I make constant modifications to improve user pleasure, sustainability and makeability.

What are the environmental implications of your work?
To use our resources responsibly and with joy.

Does your work have an impact on a social level?
Hopefully. It is a pleasure to use, it is fulfilling to make and provides a market for local timber production.

What made you start thinking about sustainability?
Lack of sustainability is profoundly ugly.

What makes a truly sustainable product?
Something that lasts, is useful, maintainable, is not exploitative of people or the environment, and that the owner wants to keep for a long time.

How can we turn manufacturers and specifiers on to sustainability?
By making the product good enough.

Do you have any words of wisdom for new designers?
Take sustainability as an intrinsically beautiful idea, not an add-on. Recognise the shallowness of most consumer-aspiration.

Where do you get your best ideas?
Through making things.

What motivates and inspires you?
The realisation that the world could be a vastly more interesting and just place – our material world has a vital contribution to make.

What was the last object you threw away?
A cheap pressure washer, having failed to fix it.

What was the last thing you fixed?
My glasses.

What is your guilty pleasure or biggest eco sin?
Not being a vegetarian.

If you could get everyone to do one thing every day, what would it be?
Stop buying things just because they are cheap.

COCOCHAIR

ALESSANDRO ZAMPIERI DESIGN

A tough and bouncy chair made entirely from renewable natural materials.

Dimensions: H 900mm x W 1120mm x D 650mm

Materials: Coconut husk coir fibres rubberized with natural latex, natural latex foam, wool textile

Tools: Saw, scissors, sewing machine

[re]strategies: [re]source

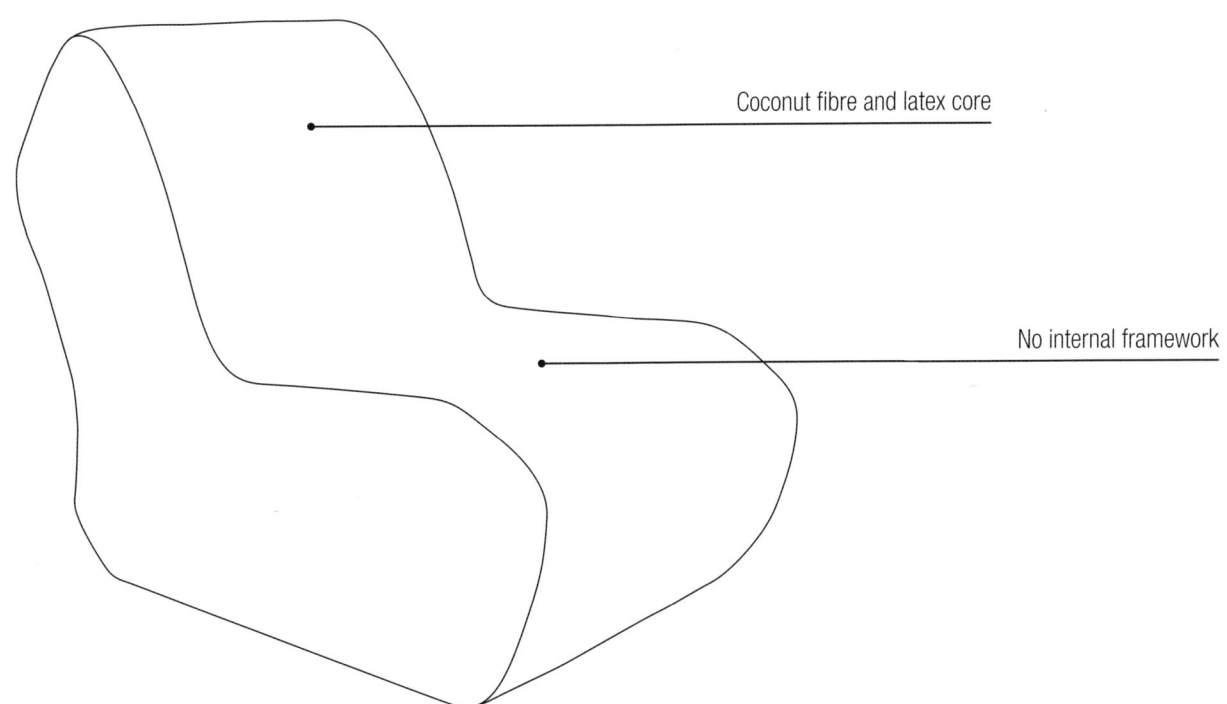

Coconut fibre and latex core

No internal framework

THE MAKING OF COCOCHAIR

[1]

[2]

[3]

[4]

The idea for Cocochair came while Alessandro was researching and experimenting with renewable natural materials for furniture. Through playing with the chair's main material – **coconut fibre sheet rubberised with natural latex [1]** – he discovered its unusual properties: resilient and durable, it can be made firmer or more flexible by altering its density or the orientation of the long curly fibres it's made from. It's an ideal natural alternative to synthetic foam for making self-supporting pieces of upholstered furniture with no internal frame.

The body of Cocochair is built from coconut fibre sheets. These are combined with latex to add resilience, before being cut to shape (using a hand saw for bespoke pieces or a mechanical saw for the mass-produced version), **sandwiched together and glued with latex [2]**.

The cushion for the seat and back is made from **natural latex foam [3]**, and the upholstery fabric is **ecologically produced wool [4]**. Natural materials like these don't make you sweat, so the chair is less susceptible to bacteria or mould than synthetic alternatives.

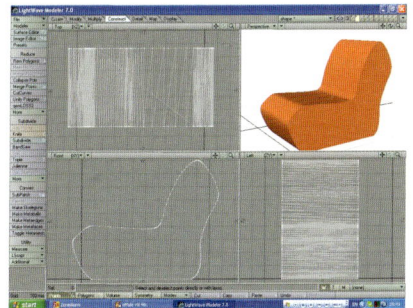

[5]

Coconut fibre comes from the husks of coconuts, so is harvested without needing to chop the trees down. It is a highly renewable resource that helps reduce carbon emissions. At the end of the chair's life the fibre can be reclaimed for use as cushion filling; it is also biodegradable, as are the latex foam and wool upholstery.

The solidity and springiness of Cocochair make it stable and tough – inviting people to use it in their own way, whether sitting, sprawling or bouncing. It can be produced as a **single seater [5]**, a modular sofa with multiple seats, or a made-to-measure piece to fit a chosen space. The design is suitable for either custom making or mass production.

IN CONVERSATION WITH ALESSANDRO ZAMPIERI

What sparked the idea for this piece?
I wanted to find a natural alternative to synthetic foam to build an upholstered product in one whole piece, without using a frame to support the shape, avoiding any need for a mould, and using a process appropriate for mass production.

What is the message behind your work?
Go natural without cutting trees down.

Do you see this design developing further? If so, how?
The material itself and the production process give great freedom to creativity but the real challenge is to design for a cheaper price… quality has a cost!

What are the environmental implications of your work?
The product uses natural and renewably sourced materials, and a low energy production process. There is an environmental cost for shipping the materials from tropical countries to Europe, but emissions are cut thanks to the fact that trees are not chopped down: we can use the coconut fibre material while keeping the coconut tree alive to absorb CO_2.

Does your work have an impact on a social level?
Coconut is a great green resource for developing countries' economies.

What made you start thinking about sustainability?
Watching nature being spoiled.

What makes a truly sustainable product?
Reduce, reuse, recycle, and most of all sustainable behaviour; there is no sustainable product without sustainable social behaviour.

How can we turn manufacturers and specifiers on to sustainability?
Managing the process as designers and bringing sustainability to the forefront of the market ourselves, then asking for the right legislation to push laziness.

…and other designers?
They should learn how to make real sustainable products, not only what is supposed to be sustainable.

Do you have any words of wisdom for new designers?
Patience.

Where do you get your best ideas?
Everywhere in life.

What motivates and inspires you?
Life and a future for the planet, but most of all mankind's future.

What was the last object you threw away?
A trolley, no longer working.

What was the last thing you fixed?
A stool.

What is your guilty pleasure or biggest eco sin?
I fly a lot.

If you could get everyone to do one thing every day, what would it be?
Take care to switch off the lights when you're not using them.

GROWNUP STOOL

CHRISTOPHER CATTLE

A simple Grow-It-Yourself three-legged stool, formed from three saplings trained and grafted to shape as they grow – inspired by the quest to make furniture using less energy.

Dimensions: H 500mm x W 400mm x D 400mm

Materials: Trees, a jig, a seat of the grower's choice

Tools: Pliers, spade, wire or plastic ties, scalpel, grafting tape, watering can, spokeshave, sandpaper

[re]strategies: [re]create [re]source

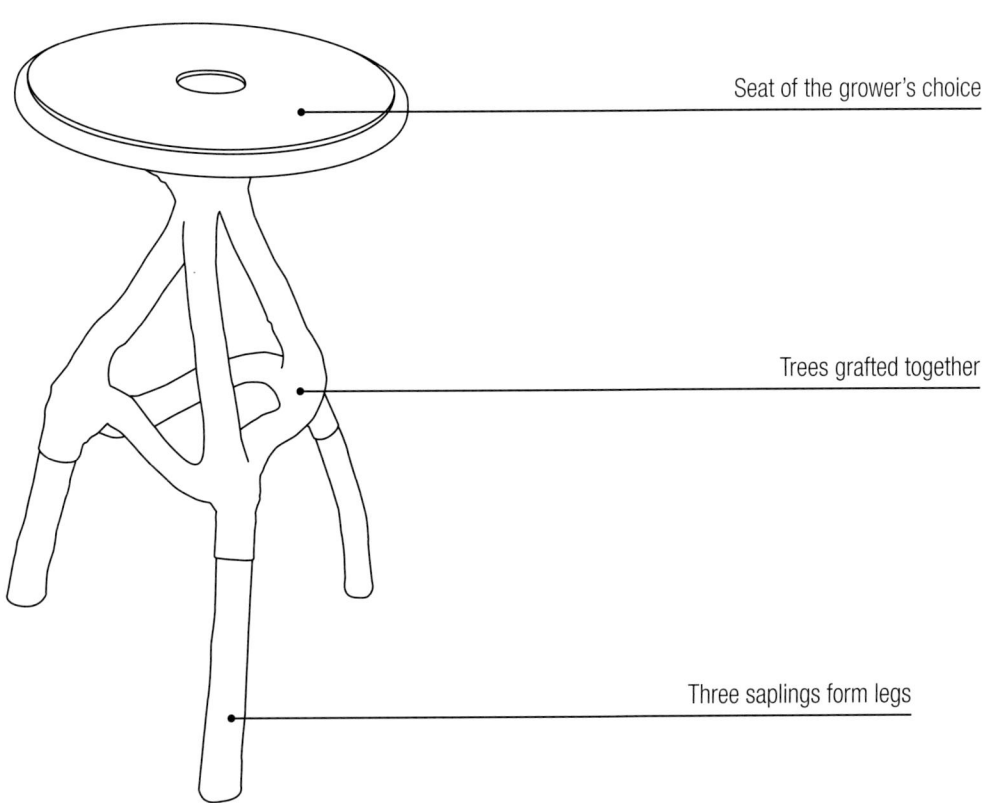

THE MAKING OF GROWNUP STOOL

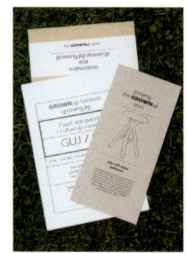
[1]
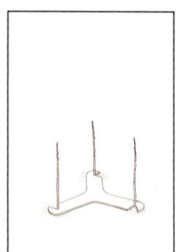
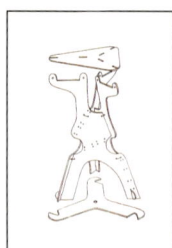
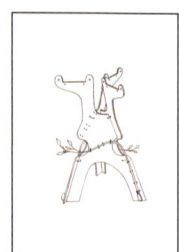

The Grownup stool grew out of Christopher Cattle's determination to find new energy-saving ways to make furniture.

As a self-generating, biodegradable material, wood was an obvious candidate for making sustainable furniture – the next step was a search for appropriate manufacturing processes and energy sources.

In the early 1990s, Christopher was aware of the annual Australian race for solar powered vehicles: "Hugely impressive in their performance, but they needed vast inputs of human time and skill and very advanced industrial technology to harness the sun's energy," he says.

Then it dawned on him that tree growth is solar powered already. The only problem, when it came to furniture, was the form that trees naturally take: "If only they grew in the right shapes in the first place, we wouldn't need so much energy to chop them up and put the bits together again." But fruit growers had been training and grafting trees into unnatural shapes for hundreds of years. Christopher decided to adapt these

[2]

[3]

[4]

[5]

well-established techniques to make simple furniture frames, and set about designing "the smallest and simplest piece of useful furniture I could devise": the Grownup stool. Years of development and practical testing proved the system's viability.

The stool is sold as a **Grow-It-Yourself instruction kit [1]**, with ready-made jigs or patterns for cutting your own jig. All that is needed is an area of reasonably **fertile ground about one metre square per stool [2]** – allowing access to all sides during growth – and three saplings of the same species (sycamore or maple are recommended).

After **training and grafting the young trees to shape [3]** over the course of about five years, the stool frame will be **ready to harvest [4]**.

It takes a further year to **air dry before adding a suitable seat [5]**. The bark may be left in place or removed, and a finish added as preferred. The process of growing makes each stool unique and intimately related to the grower.

IN CONVERSATION WITH CHRISTOPHER CATTLE

What sparked the idea for this piece?
Solar power is good – and trees use it to grow.

What is the message behind your work?
Old technologies can have new uses.

Do you see this design developing further? If so, how?
Other wooden products could surely be grown using this technique.

What are the environmental implications of your work?
Hopefully it can make people think laterally.

Does your work have an impact on a social level?
It would be nice if it did.

What made you start thinking about sustainability?
Trying to save energy.

What makes a truly sustainable product?
Nature!

How can we turn manufacturers and specifiers on to sustainability?
With great difficulty – they have too much invested in the status quo.

…and other designers?
Ditto – sadly.

Do you have any words of wisdom for new designers?
No. If they are any good they will be wiser than oldies like me.

Where do you get your best ideas?
In museums.

What motivates and inspires you?
Thinking about the world that my grandchildren will inhabit.

What was the last object you threw away?
A foil lined cardboard tube with a metal base – hard to recycle!

What is your guilty pleasure or biggest eco sin?
Using the car instead of the bike – especially when it's raining.

If you could get everyone to do one thing every day, what would it be?
Smile.

I B POP

BLUE MARMALADE

An ingeniously folded indoor or outdoor chair made from a single sheet of recycled plastic using no additional fixings.

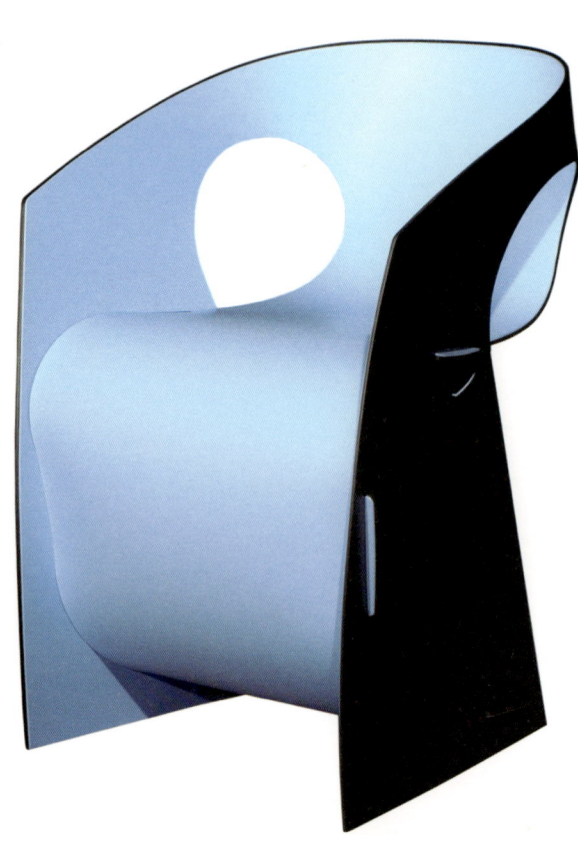

Dimensions: H 740mm x W 520mm x D 520mm

Materials: 98% recycled plastic

Tools: CNC machine

[re]strategies: [re]cycle [re]duce [re]make

Cut and folded from flat sheet

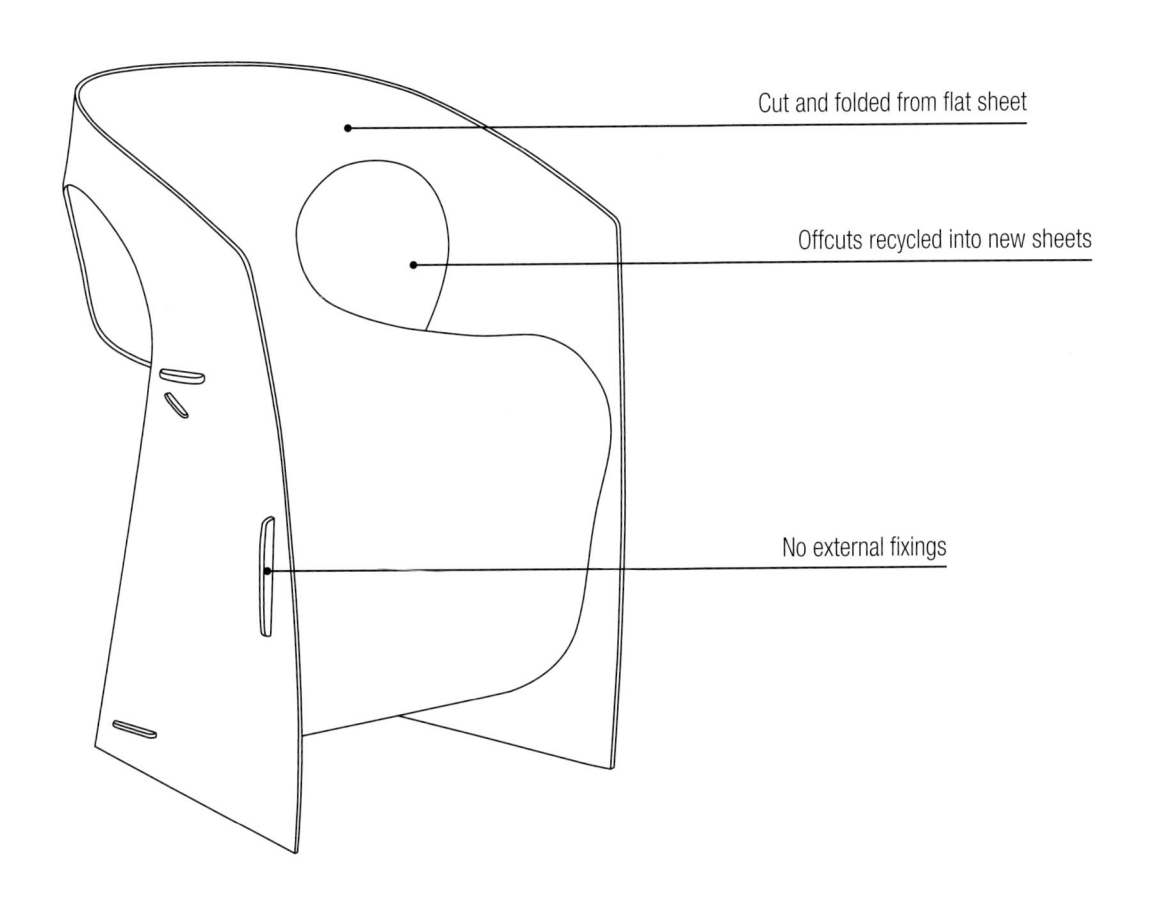

Offcuts recycled into new sheets

No external fixings

THE MAKING OF I B POP

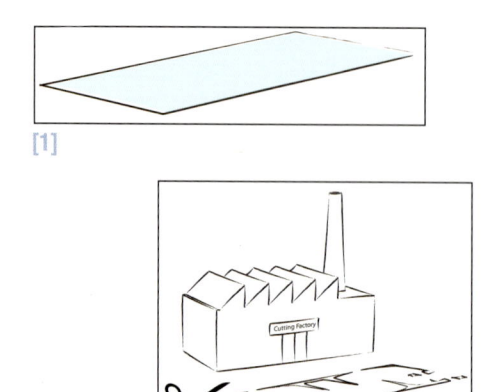

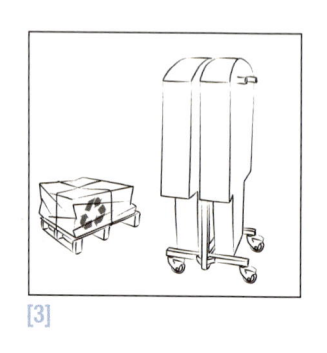

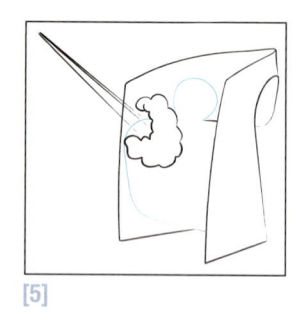

[1]

[2]

[3]

[4]

[5]

Blue Marmalade creates distinctive, colourful folded products from minimal components – in the case of the i b pop, just a **single plastic sheet [1]**, **CNC cut [2]** and hand-assembled – with no glues or additional fixings. As much of the sheet is used as possible, and larger offcuts are used to create other products, with the remainder being recycled. Manufacturing takes place close to home, mainly in the UK but also in other parts of the EU.

Blue Marmalade's 98% recycled plastic is specially made to a custom size and texture, using their own recipe that doesn't add any heavy metals or harmful chemicals. Its production is a low-energy process and it can be recycled an almost indefinite number of times. Ingredients include Blue Marmalade's own offcuts and plastic waste from other sources. As the plastic is not contaminated during production the whole chair can be recycled as is, without the need for disassembly and sorting.

i b pop has its own **vertical racking system [3]** on wheels that allows almost half a ton of chairs to be easily transported without the need for forklift trucks or other heavy machinery.

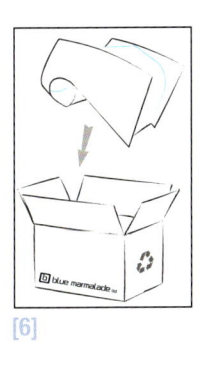

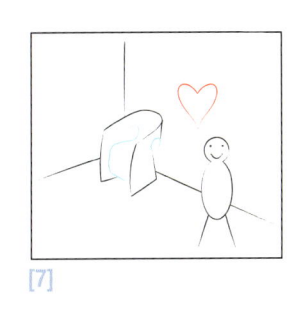

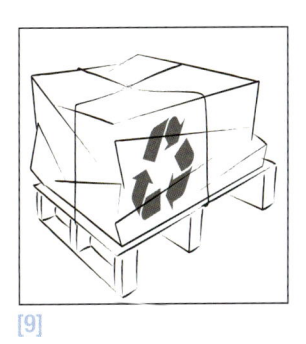

For bulk orders, i b pop chairs are sent out flat and assembled close to their destination, saving space and energy in storage and distribution. For small orders the **chairs are pre-assembled by hand [4]**, without the aid of jigs, heat or external fixings.

Blue Marmalade products are **dusted with high pressure air jet [5]**, avoiding the use of cleaning products. They are **packed in 100% recycled material [6]** that will remain fully and easily recyclable like the products themselves.

Suitable for use both inside and out, i b pop is designed to **last many years [7]**, before **being returned to Blue Marmalade [8]**. Material from production offcuts and returned products is **stockpiled [9]** until at least five tonnes is ready to be **transformed back into new recycled sheet [10]** to make new products.

IN CONVERSATION WITH BLUE MARMALADE

What sparked the idea for this piece?
To create a chair from a single flat component made from recycled plastic without using additional fixings or the use of heat.

What is the message behind your work?
Environmental impact is best addressed at the design stage with tight control of the manufacturing processes involved.

Do you see this design developing further? If so, how?
The main ongoing process is the development in the recycled plastic.

What are the environmental implications of your work?
We produce our products from recycled materials wherever we can and always use materials that are fully and easily recyclable. We design our products so that the component materials can be easily separated for recycling and we consciously design out harsh chemicals or processes. In the case of the i b pop only a single material is used, so the whole chair can be recycled as is.

The production methods we use are low energy and all happen in a relatively small geographic area to help minimise the environmental footprint. All off-cuts are used for other products or collected by us for recycling into new Blue Marmalade products so practically nothing ends up in land-fill or an incinerator.

All our packaging is made from recycled materials and is also easy to recycle.

Does your work have an impact on a social level?
We manufacture our products in the UK, so we can personally guarantee that they have been produced under socially acceptable conditions. We also like to think that combining eco-concerns with contemporary design-led products helps popularise green products to the wider public.

What made you start thinking about sustainability?
Having worked in traditional design for manufacture and exhibition design, we were very disheartened by the inefficient use of processes and the amount of waste commonly produced. We decided to set up a design practice to address those issues right from the beginning, in the design stage. This focus now follows through our entire product range and our consultancy work.

What makes a truly sustainable product?
A designer who is aware of the impact of the full life-cycle of the product he or she is designing.

How can we turn manufacturers and specifiers on to sustainability?
We need to produce goods that appeal to the consumer on the merits of their design and functionality, but are also sustainable. The consumers desire for these goods will then drive specifiers and manufacturers towards sustainable design.

…and other designers?
If there is consumer demand for sustainable products designers will provide them…

Do you have any words of wisdom for new designers?
You can make the world a better place.

Where do you get your best ideas?
On my bicycle.

What motivates and inspires you?
A job well done.

What was the last object you threw away?
A broken teapot.

What was the last thing you fixed?
A Dyson vacuum cleaner.

What is your guilty pleasure or biggest eco sin?
Air travel (counts on both fronts).

If you could get everyone to do one thing every day, what would it be?
Buy a Blue Marmalade product.

JOY

ORANGEBOX

A colourful range of task chairs designed with sustainability, comfort and quality in mind.

Dimensions: H 980mm x W 650mm x D 520mm

Materials: Polypropylene, glass reinforced nylon, steel, aluminium, natural wool, foam

Tools: Injection moulding, die casting, steel pressing, foam moulds, drills, spanner, steamer

[re]strategies: [re]cycle [re]duce [re]make

Replaceable cushions

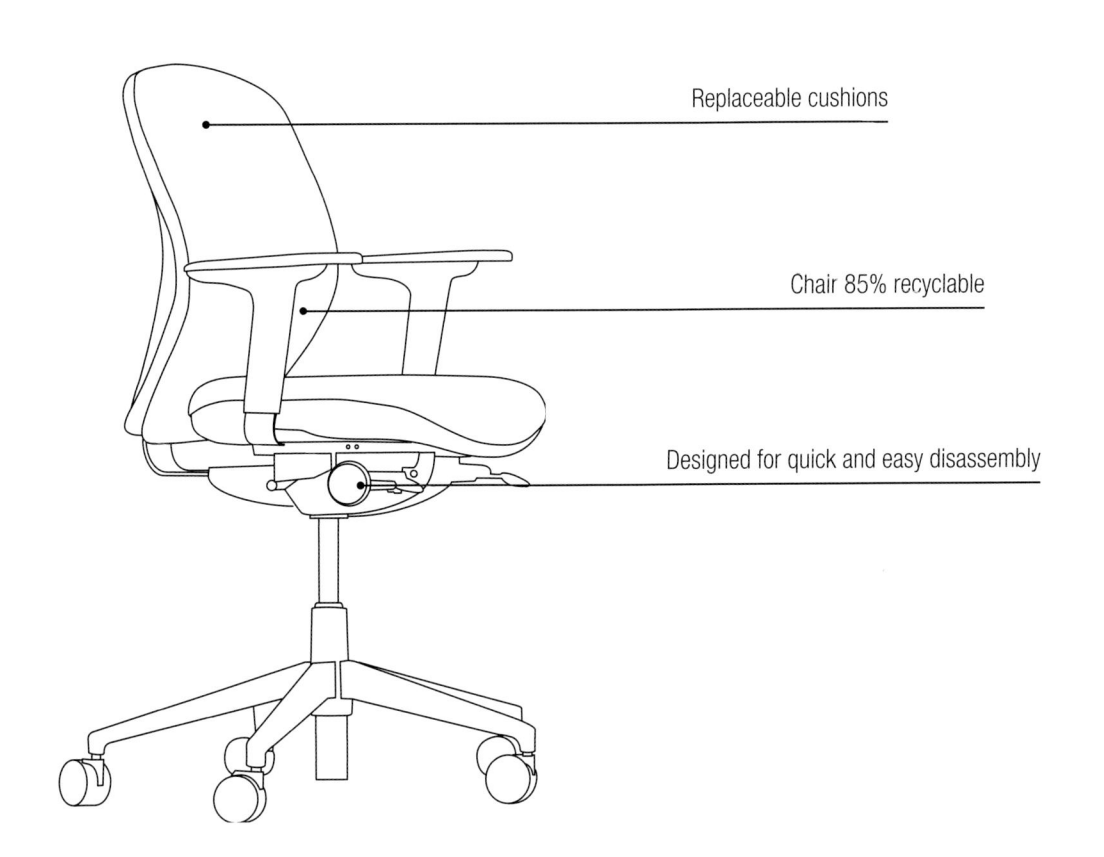

Chair 85% recyclable

Designed for quick and easy disassembly

THE MAKING OF JOY

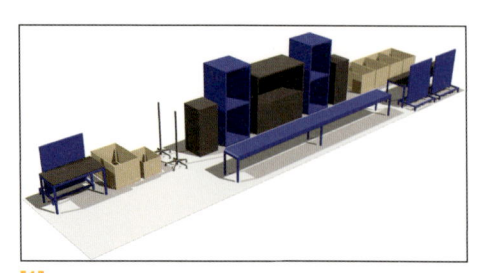

[1]

[2]

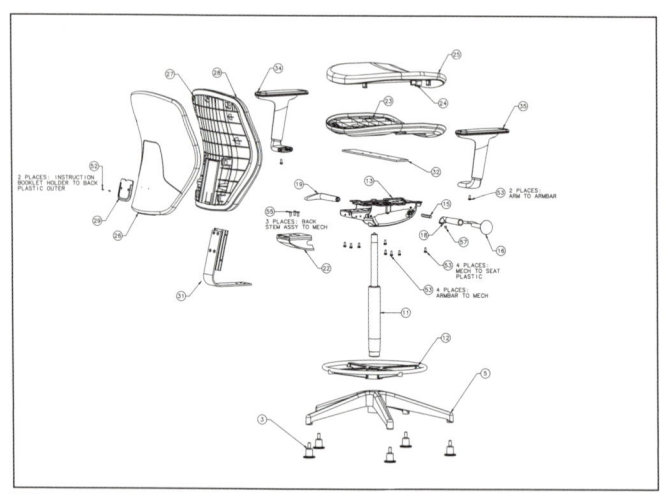

[3]

[4]

Orangebox set out to develop a competitively priced office chair which would meet customers' demands for sustainability, style and ergonomic comfort. Joy was the result, and they describe it as a "giant step forward".

The design team were responsible for developing not only the chair itself, but also its **assembly process [1]**, working closely with supply chain partners to ensure minimal environmental impact throughout its lifecycle. Orangebox was the first UK office seating manufacturer to achieve ISO14001 accreditation for environmental management.

The plastic used for the seat and back is 40% recycled [2], and the whole chair is 85% recyclable. **Designed for quick and easy disassembly [3]** for recycling, all components are labelled with material identifiers. Composite materials are eliminated, fixings are minimised and only water-based adhesives are used.

Returnable stillages [4] are used with all suppliers, cutting waste and saving costs. Component road miles are minimised by using local suppliers wherever possible.

[5]

[6]

[7]

Energy and resource efficiency have been carefully considered. Section thicknesses are minimised where possible, consuming less material and reducing weight to save energy in transportation.

The three-phase manufacture of each chair (**sub-assembly [5]**, **upholstery application [6]**, and final assembly with quality check) takes only 2 minutes 15 seconds and is highly energy efficient. 800 units are produced each week through a single assembly line with six operatives. Packaging is designed to save space, with a dedicated fleet delivering **chairs packed in poly-bags [7]** rather than boxes. All waste cardboard and polythene is recycled.

All components are designed for longevity: "Our customers are more likely to treasure and look after a product that they respect in terms of its quality and design aesthetic," say Orangebox. Joy has passed the stringent durability tests of BS1335 & BS5459 – the latter normally only associated with higher-priced chairs. Joy chairs are also upgradable, with detachable cushions that can be replaced to revive old chairs and extend their life.

IN CONVERSATION WITH ORANGEBOX

What sparked the idea for this piece?
Listening to our customers who were asking us for a product which was competitively priced without being just another cheap import from the other side of the world.

What is the message behind your work?
Keep it smart but simple.

Do you see this design developing further? If so, how?
The Joy chair has been a fantastic success in the market place and our customer base is demanding additions to the Joy range – but we're not telling you yet!

What are the environmental implications of your work?
Mass production demands environmental responsibility because we're making so much stuff!

Does your work have an impact on a social level?
Our products are designed and manufactured in Wales and that's really important to us and the local economy. They're about making people more comfortable in work by looking great and keeping them healthy.

What made you start thinking about sustainability?
This topic is no longer ignorable! As designers we're on the frontline when it comes to determining the usage of the limited resources we have available to us.

What makes a truly sustainable product?
A holistic approach to product development that looks at all the ways we use energy, from idea to end of life.

How can we turn manufacturers and specifiers on to sustainability?
By taking the lead – showing that as well as being more ethically sound, 'green' products and services can make great business sense too. We actively engage our supply chain to become ecologically responsible and our experiences show that supply chain pressure is a great incentive. Product marketing is crucial for specifiers. Sustainable design principles promote a healthier business model.

…and other designers?
Knowledge transfer through business to business networks… and get to them before they leave Uni.

Do you have any words of wisdom for new designers?
All future design opportunities will be based on true sustainable principles, think smart and steal a march on your competition.

Where do you get your best ideas?
We find them on the back of fag packets.

What motivates and inspires you?
Scaring the pants off the competition and thinking differently.

What was the last object you threw away?
Some plutonium I had kicking around.

What was the last thing you fixed?
Fixed the lamp shade in my bathroom and fitted a low energy bulb in the process.

What is your guilty pleasure or biggest eco sin?
Specifying chrome.

If you could get everyone to do one thing every day, what would it be?
Sort their rubbish out!

MAX
REESTORE

A bold and stylish, custom-upholstered retro sofa created from a vintage cast iron bath.

Dimensions: H 650mm x W 1700mm x D 700mm

Materials: Discarded roll top bath, FSC ply, reconstituted foam and thin layer of new upholstery foam, charity shop textiles

Tools: Ruler, marker, masking tape, angle grinder, spanner, hammer, paintbrush, saw, staple gun

[re]strategies: [re]mind   [re]use

Reused bath

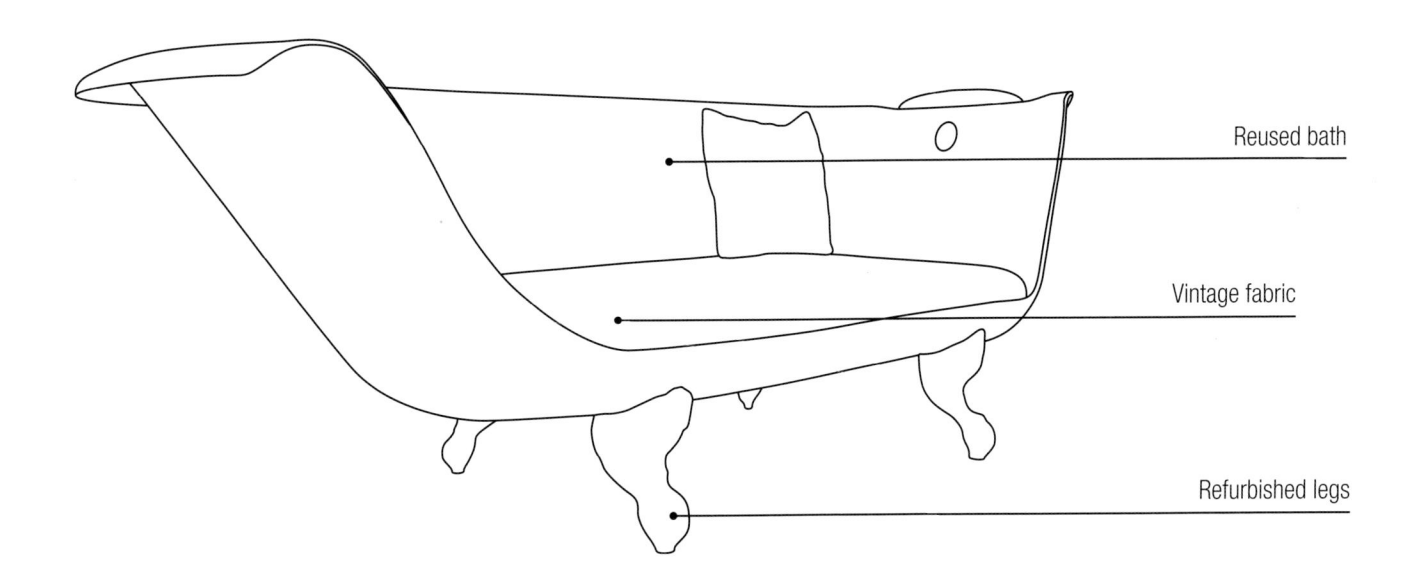

Vintage fabric

Refurbished legs

THE MAKING OF MAX

[1]

[2]

[3]

Reestore creates characterful contemporary furniture and lighting from domestic and industrial waste – communicating the message of re-use by keeping the original components clearly visible, yet **transforming them [1]** into stylish and useful new products. The range is currently extending to include an affordable modular house made from used shipping containers, combined with the latest green build techniques such as green roofing, rainwater harvesting and south-facing glazing.

A comfy addition to the contents of any eco-conscious home is the Max chaise, inspired by the sofa briefly featured in Breakfast at Tiffany's. Vintage cast iron baths – complete with roll top and ornate feet – are salvaged from scrapyards or eBay. The **feet are removed [2]** to be painted, or electroplated for a longer-lasting finish.

There is typically some chipping to bath's enamel, so **the more damaged side is removed [3]** to create the sofa shape. Cutting is done with an **angle grinder [4]**, using a stone-cutting attachment for the enamel surface, and a metal-cutting attachment for the metal body of the bath.

[4]

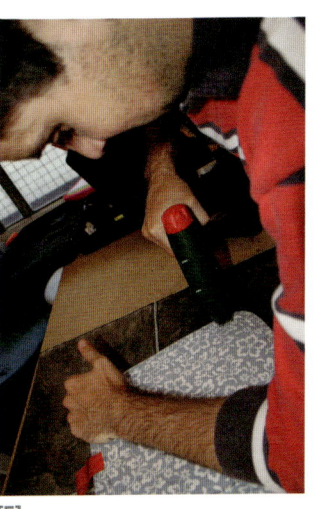

[5]

The outside is painted, and the inside enamel cleaned and touched up where necessary. Sustainably grown FSC ply is used as a base for the seat, **upholstered in reconstituted foam with a thin layer of new foam** [5].

The seat is custom-covered in suitably retro fabric, made from old curtains and other textiles sourced from charity shops. An upholstered "arm-rest" is created where the taps used to be – this varies from bath to bath, making each one slightly different. The exterior paint colour is also customisable.

Max is ideal for single-seater slouching or reclining, or a cosy sofa for two. Rubber ducks not required.

IN CONVERSATION WITH REESTORE

What sparked the idea for this piece?
Breakfast at Tiffany's and a love for loafing.

What is the message behind your work?
Look at the beauty in everyday items. Eco does not mean hemp and dirty fingernails.

Do you see this design developing further? If so, how?
The design is already extremely popular, and a limited run of 50 is to be produced by Max McMurdo for Reestore.

What are the environmental implications of your work?
Changing attitudes.

Does your work have an impact on a social level?
I'm currently building an eco living space to solve first time buying problems.

What made you start thinking about sustainability?
An inspirational 18 months living in Germany.

What makes a truly sustainable product?
Well-designed, beautiful products that consumers don't want to discard.

How can we turn manufacturers and specifiers on to sustainability?
Unfortunately they generally react to financial influences. Let's make eco design desirable and therefore profitable.

…and other designers?
It's their obligation – designers are responsible for shaping the future.

Do you have any words of wisdom for new designers?
Hang on in there.

Where do you get your best ideas?
In skips.

What motivates and inspires you?
My work is just Blue Peter on steroids. It's fun, ethical and is starting to pay.

What was the last object you threw away?
A milk carton – I separated the label from the plastic obviously.

What was the last thing you fixed?
A coffee table I bought for a fiver from a junk yard.

What is your guilty pleasure or biggest eco sin?
When I drive my Smart with the roof down. It reduces the mpg but increases my smile.

If you could get everyone to do one thing every day, what would it be?
Purchase a shopping trolley chair – oh and make world peace!

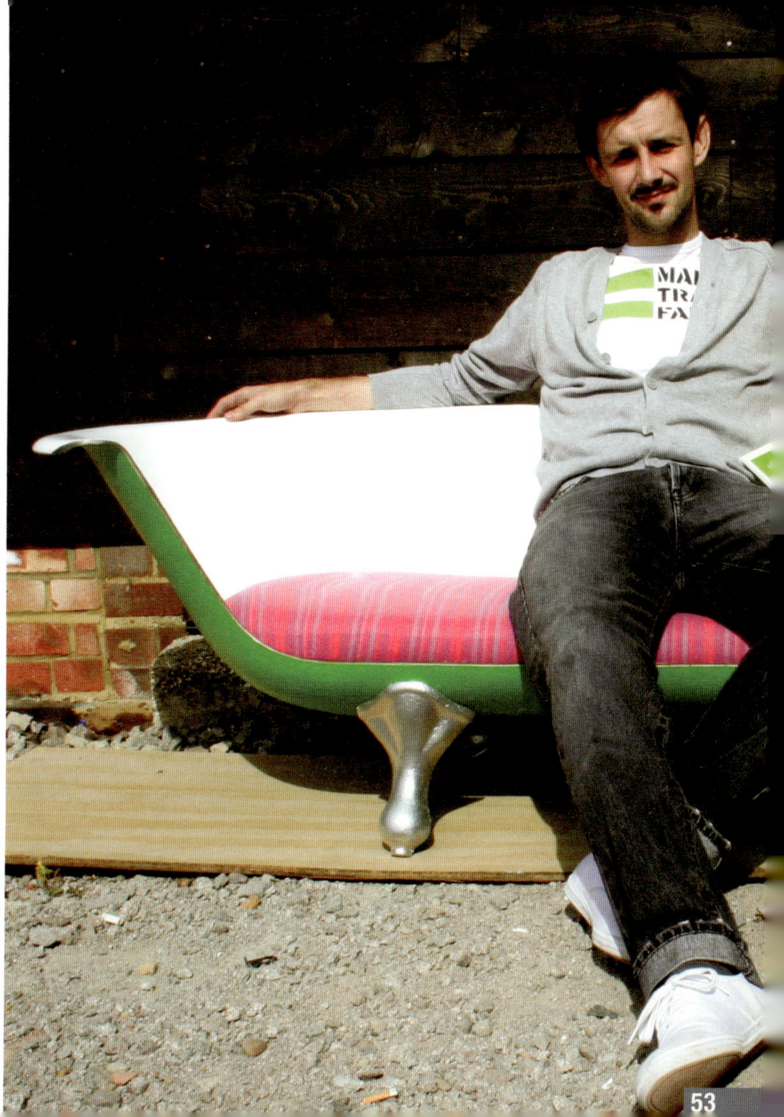

ONCE A DOOR

CLAIRE HEATHER-DANTHOIS

One of a series of sculptural seats made from reclaimed timber (in this case an old door) with steel cable giving form and flex. Commissions can make use of a client's own disused wood.

Dimensions: H 800mm x W 400mm x D 1000mm

Materials: Reclaimed wood, steel cable

Tools: Band saw, sander, drill

[re]strategies: [re]claim [re]create [re]mind

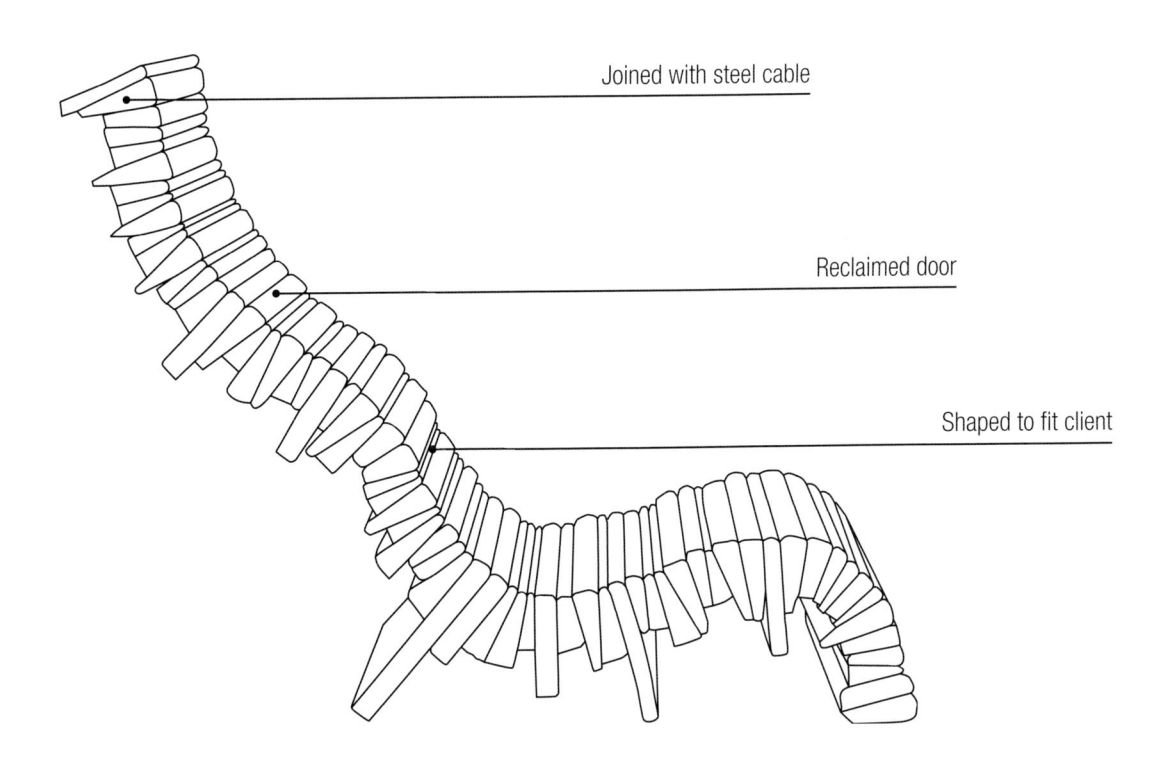

Joined with steel cable

Reclaimed door

Shaped to fit client

THE MAKING OF ONCE A DOOR

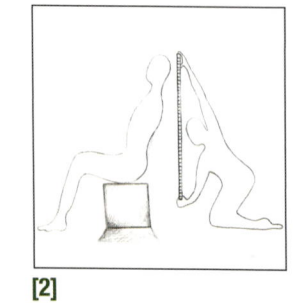

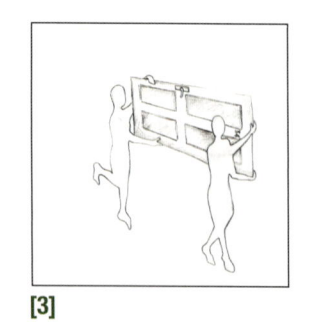

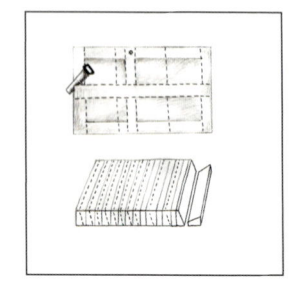

[1]

[2]

[3]

"I had always been compelled to re-use materials, as it seemed ridiculous to me to **waste things [1]** that already have so much beauty from their past existence," says Claire Heather-Danthois.

This sculptural seat combines ecological concerns with a focus on people and their relationship with the world around them: "The chair, as an object, has such a close physical relationship with a person." Exploring the area of the body that is in contact with a chair, Claire examined the interlocking forms of vertebrae in profile and simplified them until they became triangles, then extended these into a three dimensional object.

Each chair is **made to suit an individual's needs and body proportions [2]**. Each has its own character, depending on the timber (which may include **clients' own disused doors [3]** or other furniture, or wood sourced from a local reclaimed timber store) and the individual it has been created for.

Next came the search for a suitable fixing method. Glue was avoided, both

[4]

[5]

[6]

[7]

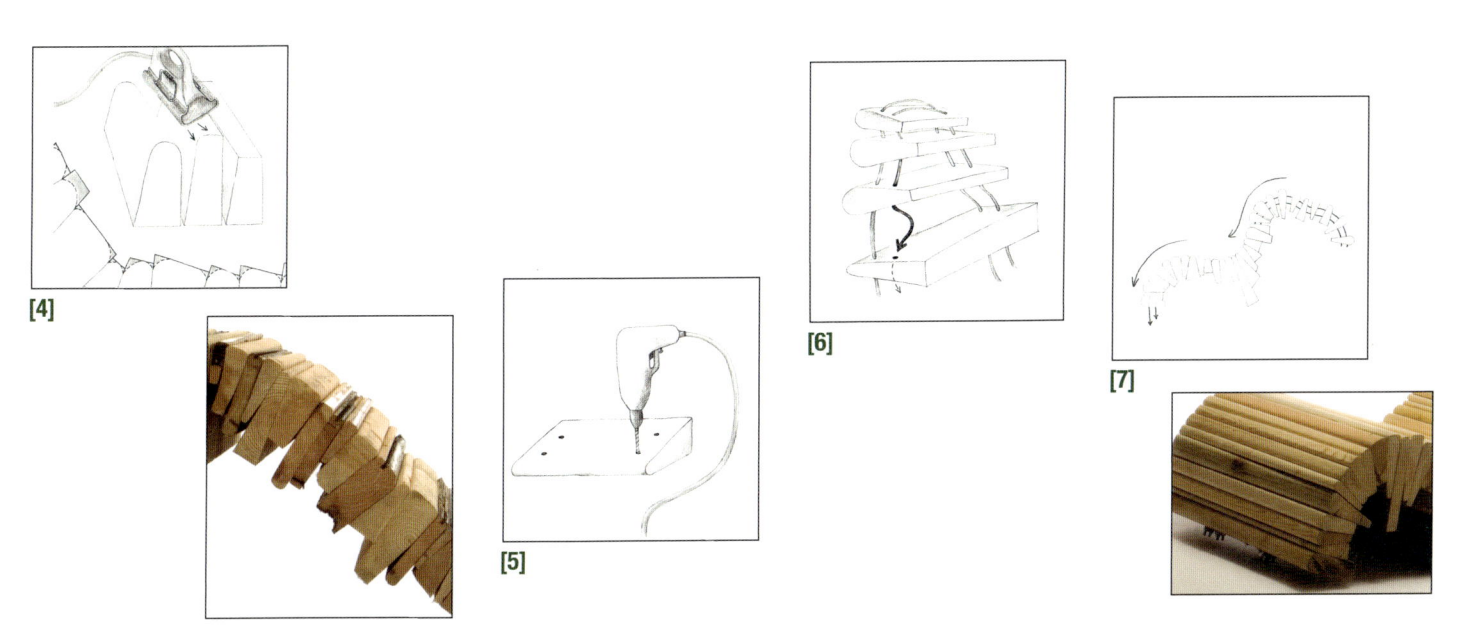

for ecological reasons and because it would make the chair completely rigid. Instead, Claire discovered that fixings used for boat rigging were ideal to cope with the massive pressure the structure would be under – and would give the seat a satisfying spring action. The use of cable also allows seat profiles to be tested and refined. Two loops of cable are threaded through four equally-spaced holes and secured at the base.

The reclaimed wood is simply **cleaned and machined [4]**, before **drilling [5], threading [6]** and **tensioning [7]**.

No finish is applied, minimising pollution and allowing the history of the timber to show. The same system can be used to create a range of long lasting, robust furniture including loungers, stools and tables.

IN CONVERSATION WITH CLAIRE HEATHER-DANTHOIS

What sparked the idea for this piece?
The human form and backbone interlocking.

What is the message behind your work?
Look what you can do with materials heading for landfill.

Do you see this design progressing? If so, how?
With every commission the form will continuously change, and there may be variations in types of wood. I would also perhaps like to see covers being made for outdoor use.

What are the environmental implications of your work?
Once a Door is made from reclaimed wood and is constructed with metal cable, using no glue!

Does it have an impact on a social level?
Encourages people to think twice before throwing away scrap wood and hopefully inspires them to use their imagination to create objects from recycled materials.

What made you start thinking about sustainability?
I have never understood why things that can be used again aren't and it brings me more satisfaction when you can see one thing be transformed into another. This was reinforced by an inspiring tutor at university.

What makes a truly sustainable product?
There is no one answer but perhaps a combination of many things including materials, method of making, using local resources etc…

How can we turn manufacturers and specifiers on to sustainability?
Try to make them see the long-term benefits rather than concentrating on making money right now.

…and other designers?
Encourage them to see sustainability as being just something they HAVE to consider.

Do you have any words of wisdom for new designers?
Teaching them that as designers it is our responsibility to take care of our planet (as a doctor would its patient) as its future is in our hands.

Where do you get your best ideas?
Walking through unfamiliar environments.

What motivates and inspires you?
People and communication – for me designing is just another way of speaking my mind.

What was the last object you threw away?
Shoes – the sole had fallen off.

What was the last thing you fixed?
The dishwasher – duck tape.

What is your guilty pleasure or biggest eco sin?
Air travel.

If you could get everyone to do one thing every day, what would it be?
Recycle all household waste!

POLY-MORPH
LOU ROTA

A distinctive update on the art of decoupage transforms a utilitarian salvaged polypropylene chair into a covetable object.

Dimensions: H 750mm x W 500mm x D 480mm

Materials: Salvaged polypropylene chair, PVA glue, paper, decoupage medium, water slide decals, ultra tough acrylic lacquer, dead flat acrylic varnish

Tools: Scissors, brushes

[re]strategies: [re]mind [re]use

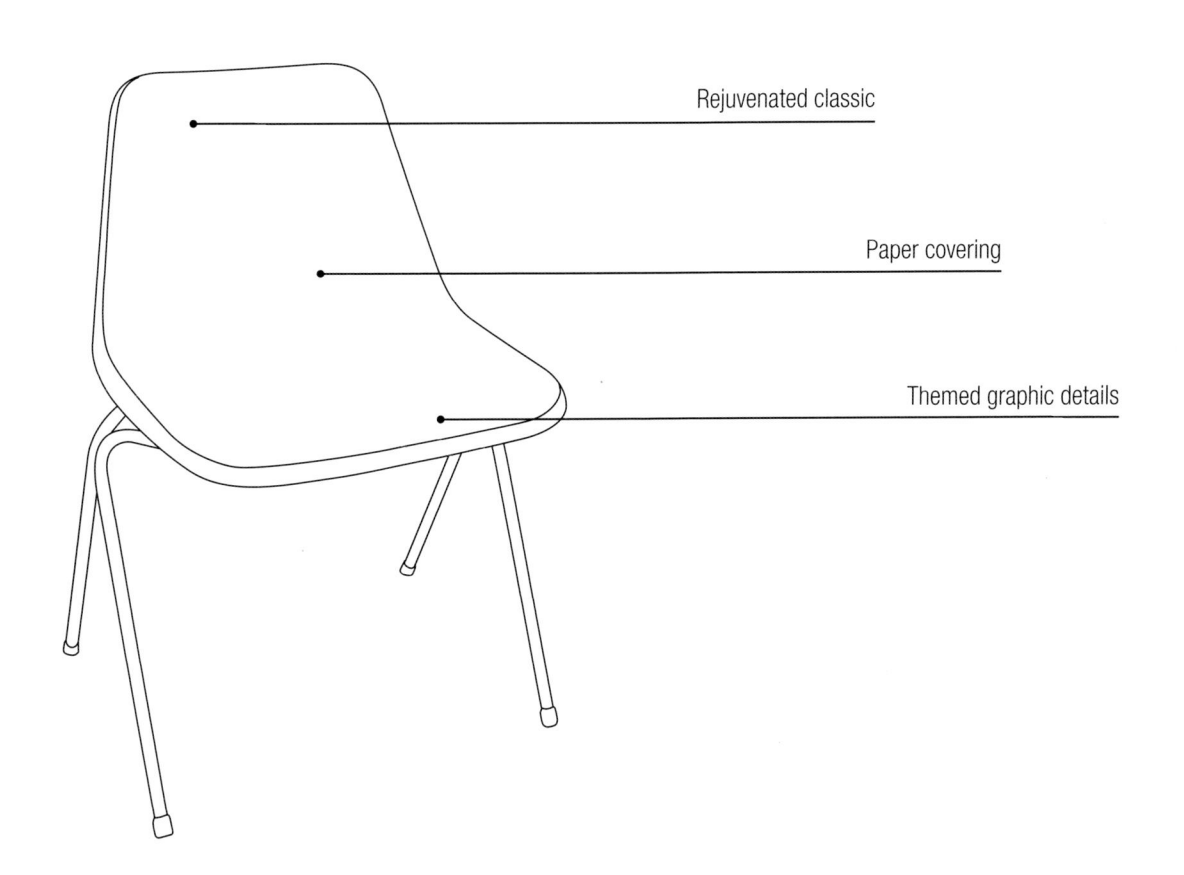

- Rejuvenated classic
- Paper covering
- Themed graphic details

THE MAKING OF POLY-MORPH

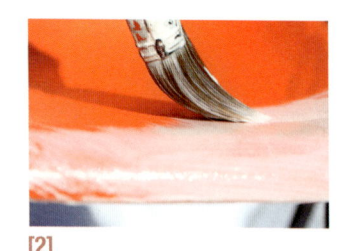

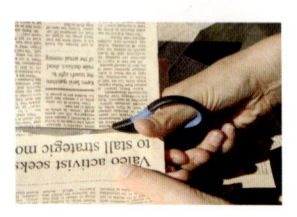

[1]

[2]

[3]

Near Lou Rota's house is a **salvage shop [1]**. Passing it every day, she'd often notice a stack of polypropylene chairs outside, unloved and unwanted. She'd think what a great shape they were, and what a shame that such a classic piece of design should have such an unglamorous image. One day she bought one: "I had an idea that I could make it into something desirable, covetable even. Give it the fairy godmother treatment."

After cleaning and priming the chair using a **PVA and water mix [2]**, she decorated it with painstakingly cut out flowers and leaves from magazines. Since then she's experimented with Amaretti papers, stamps, sweet wrappers and maps.

The Bug Chair uses a base of **plaster pink newsprint [3]**, cut into long strips about 4 cm wide. Each is coated in decoupage medium and **pasted down [4]**, gently eased into every crease and smoothed out around the contours of the chair. More strips are gradually added, all running in the same direction, emphasising the chair's undulating form.

[4]

[6]

[5]

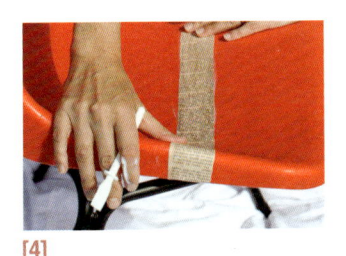

[7]

[8]

The images used to decorate the chair include Lou's own photos – "a beautiful black butterfly snapped in the rainforests of Borneo and some shiny stag beetles which the kids found at the bottom of the garden" – and others, like her **Bug Wheel [5]**, Lou designs using images from the Image Xchange, an online community of photographers.

A selection of bugs are printed or photocopied onto sheets of water-slide decal paper, cut out, and **dropped into cold water [6]** for around 60 seconds until the backing paper slides off. The transfer is then positioned **sticky side down on the chair [7]**. In this way, it's easy to create a spontaneous design – **armies of insects marching across the seat [8]** or spiders scuttling up over the back – or a more regular, wallpaper-like pattern.

Once the transfers are completely dry, the chair is finished with an ultra tough, water-based acrylic lacquer and a dead flat varnish to knock back the shine. The ubiquitous polyprop chair has become unique.

IN CONVERSATION WITH LOU ROTA

What sparked the idea for this piece?
The combination of two factors: teetering stacks of polypropylene chairs languishing in dusty corners of salvage shops, and The Conran Shop re-launching the Robin Day Polyprop chair in its Everyday Objects collection early this year.

What is the message behind your work?
Nothing new.

Do you see this design developing further? If so, how?
I'm experimenting with all manner of tired furniture and household objects.

What are the environmental implications of your work?
I'd like to think that the people who buy my chairs might otherwise have bought a brand new product.

Does your work have an impact on a social level?
Robin Day's Polyprop chair was described as one of the most democratic designs of the 20th Century. In its humble way, this re-design could be considered equally democratic. It needs no special equipment and doesn't cost much to make.

What made you start thinking about sustainability?
Landfill.

What makes a truly sustainable product?
Things that come from and eventually return to nature.

How can we turn manufacturers and specifiers on to sustainability?
It'll have to be customer demand.

…and other designers?
Same.

Do you have any words of wisdom for new designers?
Um, as one of them myself I wouldn't have the audacity!

Where do you get your best ideas?
Bed, bath, beach.

What motivates and inspires you?
Huge horizons. Rough seas. Dusty smells in foreign lands. Swimming in waterfalls. Swinging in hammocks. The souks of Marrakesh. Deep starry skies. Frosty mornings. Listening to Rufus Wainwright. Planting seeds. Picking blackberries. Junk modelling with my kids. I could go on…

What was the last object you threw away?
Some junk models. (There's only so many one house can hold.)

What was the last thing you fixed?
A pile of summer clothes.

What is your guilty pleasure or biggest eco sin?
Outdoor fairy lights. I know! I know! But they're just so darn pretty!

If you could get everyone to do one thing every day, what would it be?
To have their milk delivered in glass bottles by a friendly milkman. (Mine is called Pete and he's very nice.) Just think how much plastic that'd save.

RD4S
COHDA

The latest in Cohda's series of "Roughly Drawn" chairs, bringing a unique process and a striking new aesthetic to recycled plastic.

Dimensions: H 830mm x W 600mm x D 550mm

Materials: Domestic HDPE waste

Tools: Shredding machinery, modified industrial plastics extruder, heat-resistant hands and arms, hand-made compression tools and moulds

[re]strategies: [re]cycle [re]duce [re]make

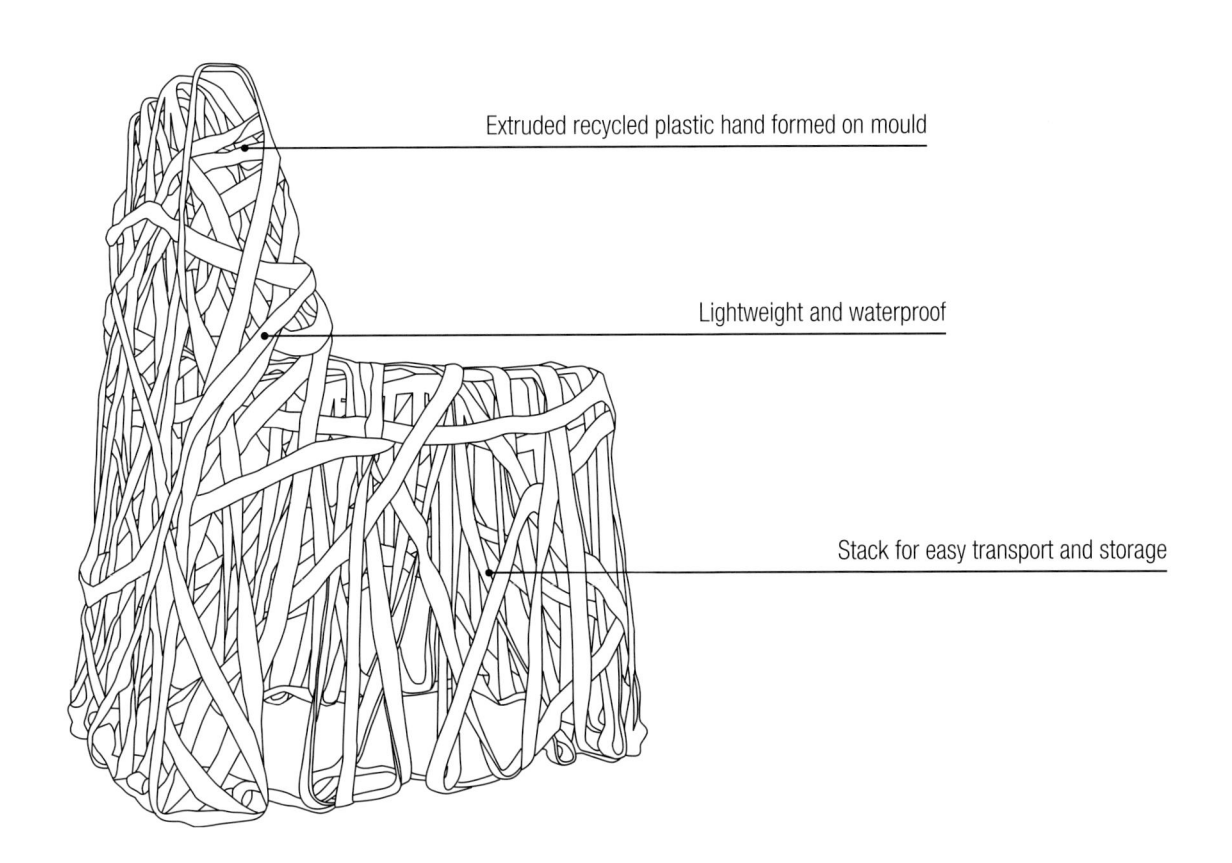

Extruded recycled plastic hand formed on mould

Lightweight and waterproof

Stack for easy transport and storage

THE MAKING OF RD4S

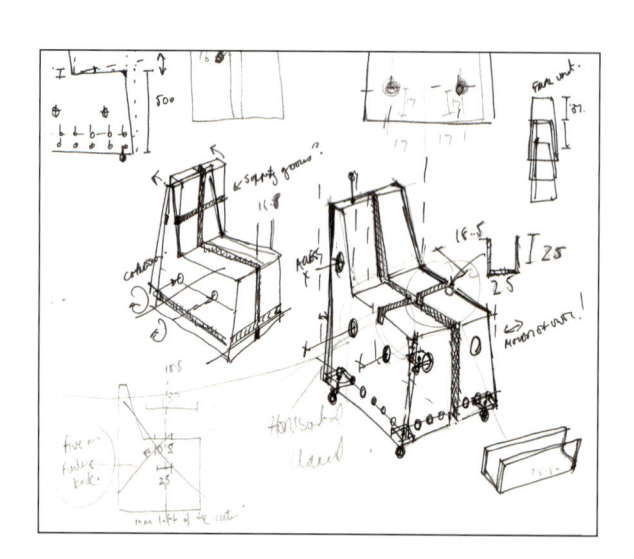

[1]

[2]

[3]

The Uncooled Recycled Extrude (URE) process – the result of a two year research project into the use of waste plastics in design – uses modified industrial plastics machinery to transform waste polymers into sculptural chairs. It breaks away from reliance on readymade recycled plastic sheet or lumber, instead allowing Cohda to work directly with plastic waste.

Domestic HDPE (high density polyethylene) [1] is an abundant raw ingredient – millions of tonnes are disposed of each year in the UK. The first step in the URE process is washing discarded bottles, bags and food trays and removing traces of labels, before shredding them to make a usable **flake material [2]**. Colour variations may be created by selecting and mixing waste, or by adding pigments (1-2%) to produce a more uniform colour.

The flake material is heated in Cohda's modified **extruder [3]** until molten. The resulting extruded ribbon of recycled plastic is **hand woven [4]** around a purpose-designed template which is engineered to allow the plastic to shrink and deform as it hardens. After cooling and removing from

[4]

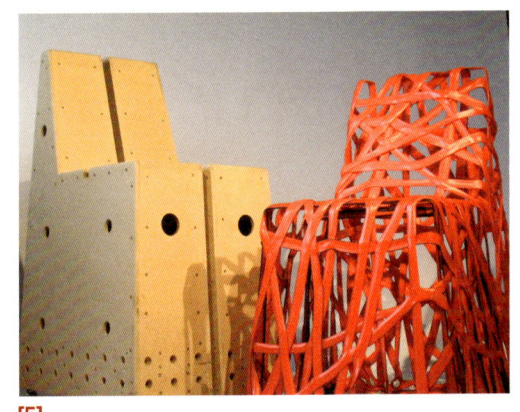

[5]

[6]

the mould, the result is a **rigid yet flexible chair [5]**.

URE eliminates several stages of the conventional recycling process, which also often involves transportation overseas. Total energy savings are high compared to typical virgin plastic alternatives (estimated at 89kwh per chair – enough saved energy to run a 60w light for 2 months continually; equivalent to saving over 38kg of CO_2 emissions).

The RD4s is **designed to stack [6]**, saving space and energy in transportation. Being made from a single material with no additional fixings, fittings or adhesives, the chair can be recycled repeatedly.

The URE process also makes a compelling and educational live performance, a "public recycling factory" where visitors can bring along their own plastic waste to be transformed into furniture, stimulating debate around issues of waste, energy and design.

IN CONVERSATION WITH COHDA

What sparked the idea for this piece?
Transportation issues related to the previous (non-stacking) RD4 design and the need to constantly reduce the product's embodied energy.

What is the message behind your work?
Recycled plastic furniture designs don't need to be restricted to sheet materials and flat pack construction.

Do you see this design developing further? If so, how?
This design is constantly being amended and developed, with the aim of making the piece as environmentally sound as possible.

What are the environmental implications of your work?
The aim is to view waste material in a more metamorphic manner whilst transporting and processing the raw waste materials as little as possible. By extracting the embodied energy in the waste and reducing the amount of useable plastic heading for landfill, energy and waste savings can be vast.

Does your work have an impact on a social level?
YES! I'll let you figure them out.

What made you start thinking about sustainability?
Frustration and absinthe.

What makes a truly sustainable product?
1- A product produced from what has previously been deemed waste.
2- A product brought into existence using as minimal an amount of energy as possible.
3- A product that can be further recycled after its second use.
4- A product that attracts public interest and generates sales.

How can we turn manufacturers and specifiers on to sustainability?
Public pressure to change. Or, take-back schemes imposed by Government and European legislation.

…and other designers?
If a designer in 2007 isn't taking into account sustainability issues in their work then they won't be working much in the next few years.

Do you have any words of wisdom for new designers?
The most interesting design opportunities are always the most difficult to develop.

Where do you get your best ideas?
Whilst travelling.

What motivates and inspires you?
The thought of what's just around the corner.

What was the last object you threw away?
A boomerang.

What was the last thing you fixed?
A friend's washing machine pump fixed with a spoon handle.

What is your guilty pleasure or biggest eco sin?
Mobile phones. I do recycle them, but I seem to be able to destroy a mobile phone by just looking at it. I'm on a mission to find an indestructible one.

If you could get everyone to do one thing every day, what would it be?
Remove the tops from plastic bottles prior to recycling. You have no idea how much energy this would save. Air doesn't weigh much! But is expensive to transport.

REEE® CHAIR

PLI DESIGN

An ergonomic, stylish stacking chair, made with recycled computer games consoles – diverting 2.4kg of plastic from landfill.

Dimensions: H 800mm x W 470mm x D 560mm

Materials: Recycled games console casing, powder-coated steel

Tools: CNC tube bending & welding, injection-moulding

[re]strategies: [re]cycle [re]make

Snap-on components for easy assembly

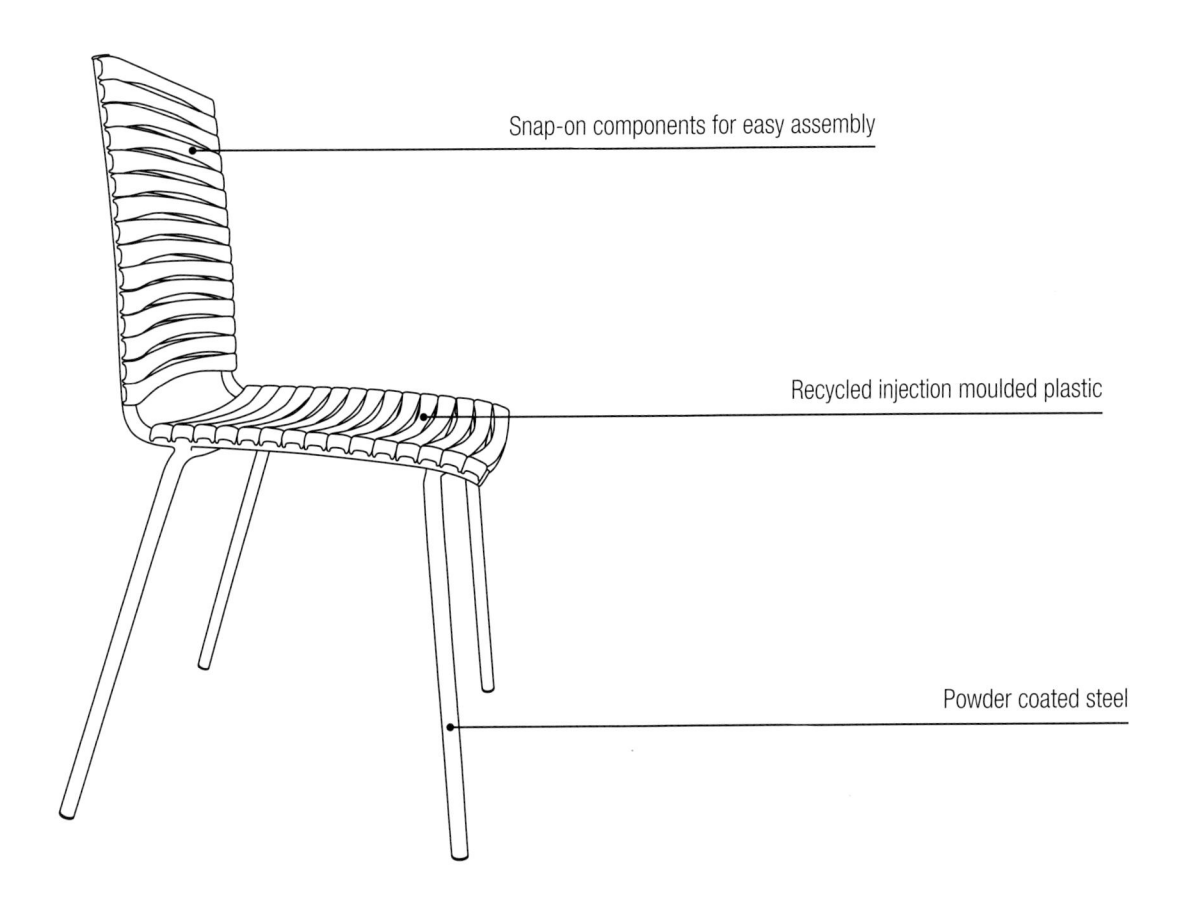

Recycled injection moulded plastic

Powder coated steel

THE MAKING OF REEE® CHAIR

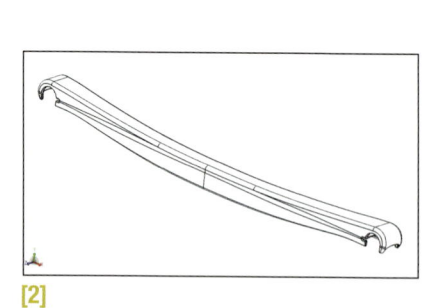

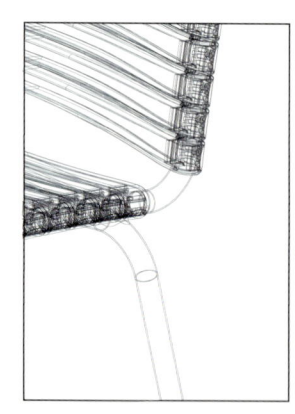

[1]

[2]

The Reee Chair was created in response to customers' requests for a truly sustainable chair suitable for homes, schools and offices – at the same time as the Europe-wide WEEE (Waste Electrical and Electronic Equipment) Directive made manufacturers responsible for taking back and recycling products at end of life.

PLI spotted an opportunity to meet both needs with one product – a chair made from recycled computer games console casings which is suitable for contract and domestic interiors. PLI commissioned the sustainable design consultancy Sprout to create a chair that would meet the challenges of a new supply chain and new customer needs.

The Reee chair aims to stimulate the market for recycled materials by highlighting new material streams and showing how their performance and durability can be maintained through more than one product lifespan. The plastic used for the seat, back and fixings is all from the same high-quality source – **used computer games console casings [1]** – which can be recycled again and again.

[3]

The future of every part of the chair has been considered: **individual ribs can be removed and replaced if damaged [2]**, allowing the chair to be repaired at low cost and increasing its useful life. At end of life the chair separates out into single source recycled plastic and a **steel frame [3]**, for further recycling or reconditioning.

It takes less energy to reprocess used plastic than to extract and process virgin plastic from crude oil. The chair is produced in the UK from UK-sourced materials, reducing both its carbon footprint and the costs of transportation and distribution. The Reee chair is priced competitively with other chair designs made from virgin plastic. Its attentive angle also encourages healthy posture through ergonomic design.

Its message is subtly brought home to anyone paying attention to the back of the chair in front – the ribs read: "Recycle again… and again… and again…"

IN CONVERSATION WITH PLI DESIGN

What sparked the idea for this piece?
PLI was in touch with two very different organisations whose needs seemed to coincide: a secondary school that needed sustainable seating to go in its new eco-designed assembly hall and an electronics manufacturer that needed to find a good home for its used computer games consoles. We thought we could meet both needs with one product – a chair made from recycled computer games console casings which is suitable for contract and domestic interiors that are also 'green spaces'.

What is the message behind your work?
You don't have to compromise on quality or price if you want to own products made from sustainable materials which also look beautiful. PLI's motivation as a business is to lead sustainable product development in light manufacturing industry – in the UK and overseas – and so to expand the market for sustainable products.

Do you see this design developing further? If so, how?
We're working with the designers, Sprout, on more products under the Reee® brand – recycled materials from 'waste' electric and electronic equipment under the WEEE directive, except it isn't waste to us. It's a new and versatile material stream.

What made you start thinking about sustainability?
If you have your eyes and ears open, you can't avoid it. Sustainability is a seam running through just about every social and business issue we're dealing with today.

What makes a truly sustainable product?
That's easy - good design makes a truly sustainable product. That's design that doesn't lose interest halfway through and forget about durability, reuse, recycling, environmental hazards or simple beauty. We wanted Sprout to design the Reee® chair because they intuitively understand responsible design.

How can we turn manufacturers and specifiers on to sustainability?
The customer is already turning specifiers on to sustainability – it's up to us manufacturers to respond and give the specifiers better options.

…and other designers?
So many designers we meet are keen on sustainable design or have some experience but so few are making sustainable design central to their practice. You're less likely to compromise if you're open about your aims and intentions regarding sustainability. If we can develop world-class professional resources to support sustainable design in the UK, the design community will grab them with both hands.

Do you have any words of wisdom for new designers?
Spend time on the factory floor, in the recycling yard, the sawmill, the facilities maintenance workshop, wherever you can. Talk to the people who are going to bring your designs to life, ask them what they reckon, make their job easier and more satisfying.

Where do you get your best ideas?
I get all my best ideas from listening to people and asking stupid questions.

What motivates and inspires you?
The Eden Project, bamboo, William McDonough and Michael Braungart (authors of "Cradle-to-Cradle"), the idea of helping to expand the market for renewable and sustainable materials.

What was the last object you threw away?
My old iBook – when it died it actually had sparks and smoke coming out of it.

What was the last thing you fixed?
Probably the bandsaw – it breaks down a lot.

What is your guilty pleasure or biggest eco sin?
Beaching that oil tanker in the Galapagos.

If you could get everyone to do one thing every day, what would it be?
Drink clean water.

ROCKY THE ROCKING SHEEP

SAM MURAT

Fun rocking sheep that promotes the use of sheepskin, a luxurious local resource.

Dimensions: H 530mm x W 650mm x L 1000mm

Materials: British 'yeti' sheepskin, European Ash

Tools: Handsaw, chisels, sewing equipment, Shopsmith: table saw, bandsaw, lathe, sanding disc, vertical drilling machine

[re]strategies: [re]source [re]spond

British sheepskin

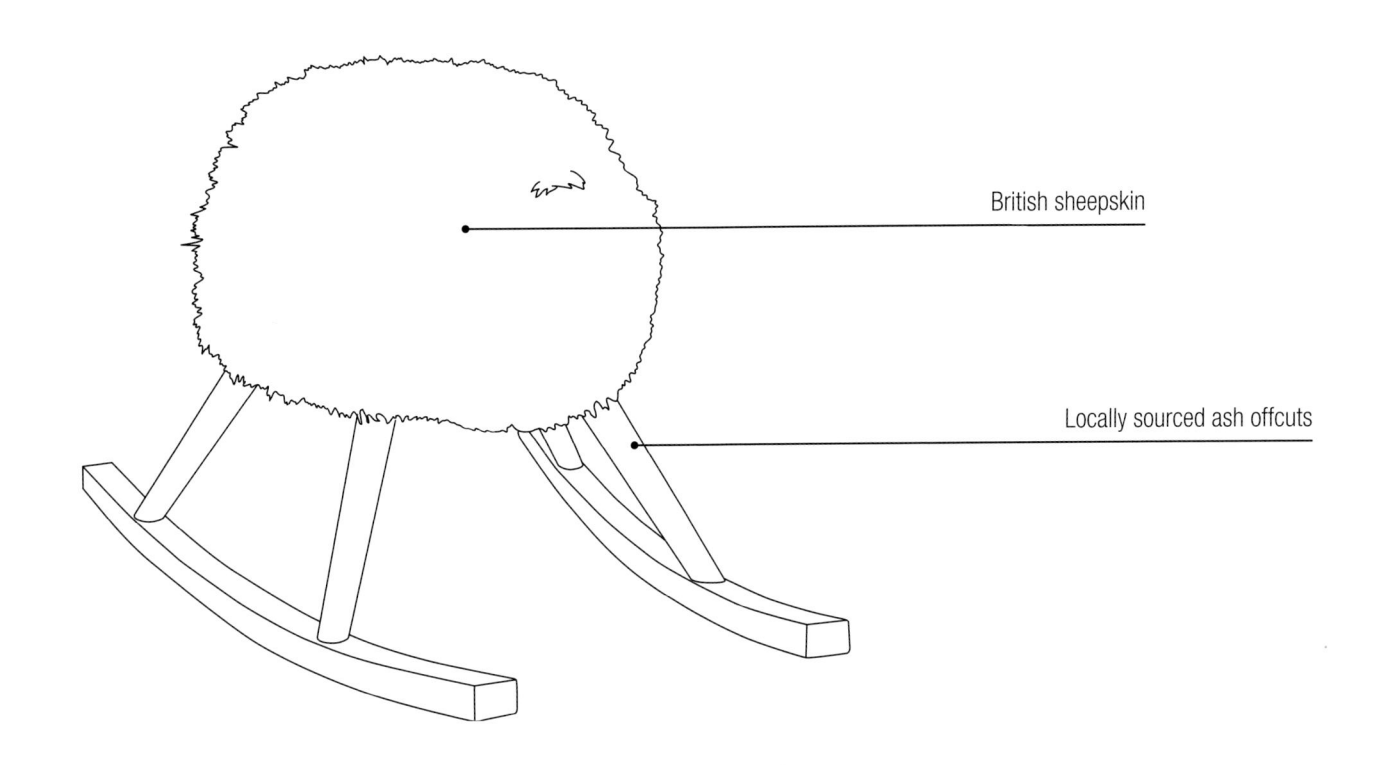

Locally sourced ash offcuts

THE MAKING OF ROCKY THE ROCKING SHEEP

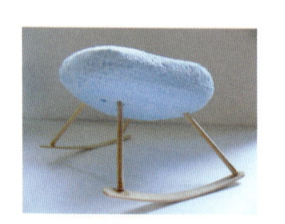

[1]

[2]

In her final year on the University of Plymouth's Designer Maker course, Sam's heart was set on making a rocking chair – when her attention was caught by a lecture from Andrew Tinnion, supported by the Real Sheepskin Association, and a visit to his tannery.

Sam's interest in sustainability had been growing throughout her studies, so she was drawn to locally produced materials which would reduce her designs' carbon footprint and support the local economy. This, in combination with sheepskin's other qualities – its luxurious feel, durability, and fire retardance – sparked her interest in sheepskin.

Sheepskin is an abundant by-product of the meat industry, but markets for it have been declining. The sheepskin used is selected for its especially long, soft and crimped texture – a result of breed and finishing techniques.

"I wanted Rocky to be **fun and have its own unique character [1]**, without becoming too much of a stereotype," says Sam. "My most successful designs to date were those that appeared to be simple."

[3]

[4]

[5]

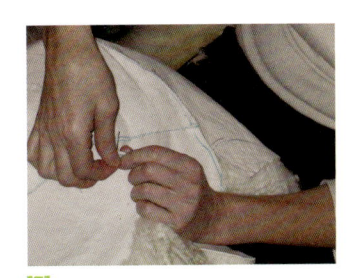

[6]

Ash, a hard close-grained wood that grows natively in the UK, was chosen for the legs and rockers – made using offcuts from Sam's local wood merchants. The rockers are routed and shaped without requiring bending. The legs are **turned to a tapered shape** [2], joined with **mortise and tenon joints** [3] at the top to make an A-frame structure.

An egg-shaped wooden seat is mounted on top. In the first version firm upholstery foam (layered and carved to shape) has been used to cover it; recycled chip foam or wool waste are possible future alternatives. A fabric template of the **seat form** [4] enables the sheepskin to be cut and **sewn** [5] to the required shape. A **linen under-cover** [6] is made to cover the seat before tacking on the sheepskin. Offcuts from the sheepskin are used to make floor cushions.

IN CONVERSATION WITH SAM MURAT

What sparked the idea for this piece?
I wanted to try and help promote the declining sheepskin industry in the UK.

What is the message behind your work?
There are lots of traditional locally available materials such as sheepskin and wood that are ideal for sustainable designs.

Do you see this design developing further? If so, how?
Yes, so far Rocky has developed into five designs in the Grazing Sheep collection, two rockers and three stools. I'm also planning an additional design with a backrest. I would like to try using Elm saplings, which have been blighted by Dutch Elm Disease, from hedgerows as a source of timber.

What are the environmental implications of your work?
With over 35 million sheep in the UK, British sheepskin is ultimately a renewable and abundant everyday by-product of the meat industry. I source locally from a tannery in the South West. Selecting timber and upholstery materials responsibly and using a natural finish for the legs is also part of ensuring a low environmental impact.

Does your work have an impact on a social level?
I believe so, even if it just raises a smile, thought or comment. I love watching people of all ages having fun interacting with my work.

What made you start thinking about sustainability?
My tutors, Roy Tam and Asaf Tolkovsky, on the Designer Maker course at The University of Plymouth really encouraged thinking about sustainability. Working on my dissertation entitled 'Sustainable Challenges' helped crystallize my own views on the subject and I soon realised the importance of working in a sustainable way.

What makes a truly sustainable product?
Locally sourced and made and a product that will be treasured and cherished for at least one lifetime but preferably longer.

How can we turn manufacturers and specifiers on to sustainability?
By legislation and making businesses responsible for the recycling and disposal of their products.

…and other designers?
I think whilst the public continue to support environmentally friendly products, designers will start to think and work differently.

Do you have any words of wisdom for new designers?
To be honest I'm a new designer myself, but if I'd give any advice it would be not to procrastinate over your ideas, just get cracking and turn them out, that way you get lots of hands on experience and learn very quickly whether the idea is feasible or not.

Where do you get your best ideas?
Lots of daydreaming and model making. I never really switch off.

What motivates and inspires you?
A captivating brief and becoming emotionally attached to a project or idea.

What was the last object you threw away?
I work on the principle of reduce, reuse, recycle but occasionally something creates a challenge. The most recent item was a broken plant pot.

What was the last thing you fixed?
A jacket lining, the inside pocket had a big hole above it.

What is your guilty pleasure or biggest eco sin?
Cooking on an Aga, but they do last forever!

If you could get everyone to do one thing every day, what would it be?
Supermarket packaging really aggravates me, my recycle bin is always bursting at the seams, so I would ask everyone to try and avoid buying something that's beautifully wrapped in a plastic film or box.

TEDDY BAG

ANDREW MILLAR

A multifunctional felt bag which becomes a comfy chair when stuffed with old clothes or soft toys.

Dimensions: H 700mm x W 350mm x D 350mm

Materials: 5mm 100% wool felt, wool thread

Tools: Die cutter, industrial sewing machine

[re]strategies: [re]duce [re]source [re]spond

Handles for easy manoeuvrability

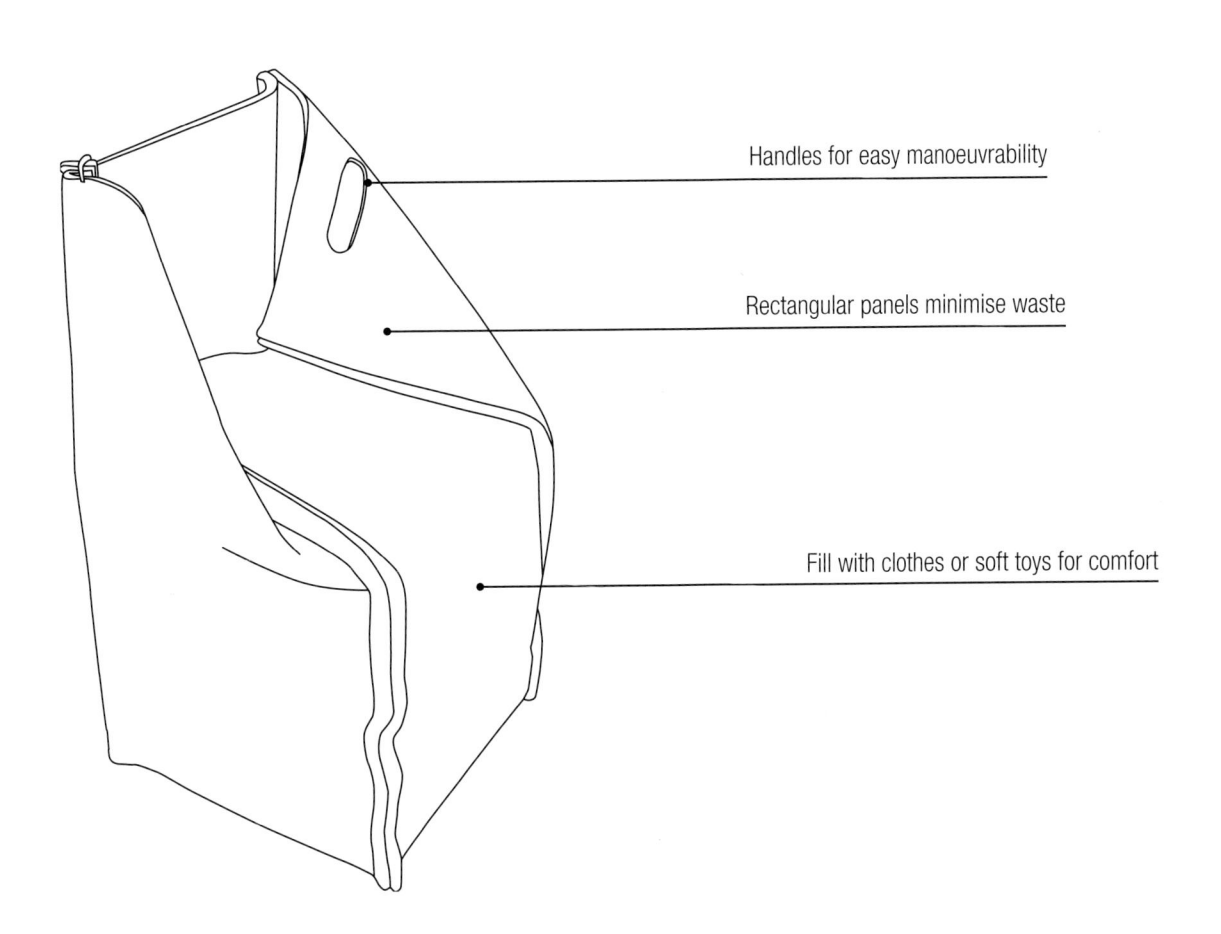

Rectangular panels minimise waste

Fill with clothes or soft toys for comfort

THE MAKING OF TEDDY BAG

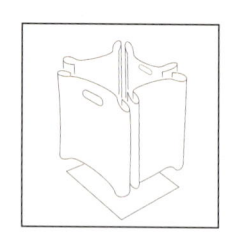

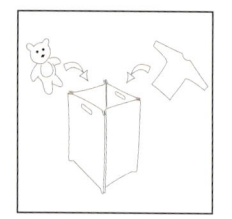

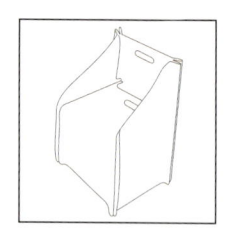

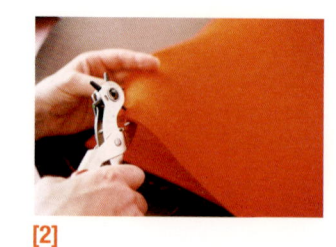

[1]

[2]

Teddy Bag was inspired by a newspaper article on how industrialised nations damage the economies of poorer countries by flooding them with donated clothing – ever more abundant as super-cheap high street clothing is perceived as disposable. The high demand for second-hand western clothes in developing countries puts local companies producing and selling traditional clothing out of business.

At the same time Andrew Millar noticed that discarded soft toys are often available at boot sales, and many of us have a box of them in the attic.

These stories of teddies and clothes got him thinking about how we could take responsibility for our own waste – by sitting on it.

Teddy Bag is a multifunctional product made from four equal-sized diecut side pieces of **5mm thick wool felt [1]**, and one square base piece, stitch fabricated together with wool using an industrial sewing machine (or in the prototype version, **hand-sewn after hole-stamping every 15mm [2]**). The labels are **laser cut and sewn in [3]**.

[3]

[4]

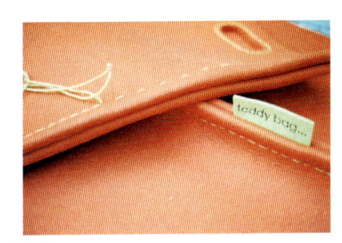

[5]

[6]

Using only rectangles allows easy shape tiling, minimising waste. Colours include orange, green, purple and natural grey. Felt is a natural product and can be recycled at end of life.

The design can be used as a **bag [4]**, **laundry basket [5]**, chair, or on its side like a beanbag. Its handles make it easily **portable [6]**.

Users are involved in creating the chair by reusing their old toys or clothes (or storing those they use). Depositing items inside the bag makes it increasingly comfortable and sturdy, encouraging the habit of reuse and resourcefulness. But overfilling it prevents its use as a chair – raising awareness of the consequences of producing too much waste.

IN CONVERSATION WITH ANDREW MILLAR

What sparked the idea for this piece?
An article on the downside of the cheap clothing retail.

What is the message behind your work?
Reduce and reuse, valuing what we have, by "sitting on our own waste," taking responsibility for what we produce, rather than sending it abroad.

Do you see this design developing further? If so, how?
Manufacture.

What are the environmental implications of your work?
Encourage users to reuse and value what they already have.

Does your work have an impact on a social level?
Hopefully!

What made you start thinking about sustainability?
An early project whilst studying, in which I came across "Design for the Real World" by Victor Papanek.

What makes a truly sustainable product?
Local sourcing, local production, local distribution, local consumption, linked with natural materials creates truly sustainable products.

How can we turn manufacturers and specifiers on to sustainability?
We need to make them believe in the cause, not just "jump on the bandwagon" due to increased consumer awareness and media pressure.

…and other designers?
Pass on a copy of Design for the Real World - bleak stuff!

Do you have any words of wisdom for new designers?
I myself am a new designer!

Where do you get your best ideas?
Walking through the City, visiting markets, lazing in a park, sitting in a café…

What motivates and inspires you?
Trying to make a difference and contribute towards a solution.

What was the last object you threw away?
Battered pair of trainers, they had their fair share of use!

What was the last thing you fixed?
My car… good or bad!?

What is your guilty pleasure or biggest eco sin?
I enjoy driving on long car journeys, and I like to travel abroad (by plane!)

If you could get everyone to do one thing every day, what would it be?
Reuse something.

TETRIS
WEMAKE

A Make It Yourself inspiration kit – using discarded cardboard boxes to create the world's cheapest designer furniture.

Dimensions: H 700mm x W variable x D 1100mm

Materials: Cardboard, PVA glue

Tools: Pencil, metal ruler, scissors or craft knife, cutting mat, brush

[re]strategies: [re]claim [re]create

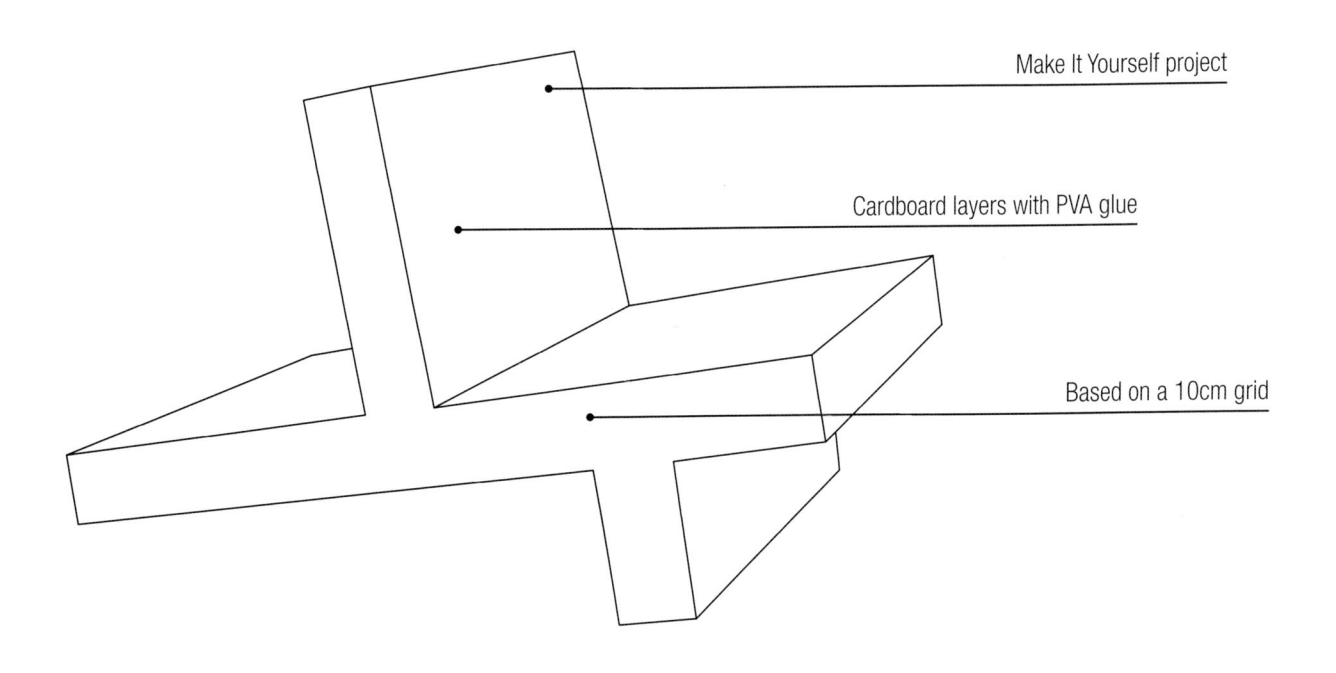

Make It Yourself project

Cardboard layers with PVA glue

Based on a 10cm grid

THE MAKING OF TETRIS

[1]

[2]

[3]

[4]

Tetris is a modular furniture system based on a 10cm grid, which encourages people to reuse **discarded cardboard packaging [1]** to make their own furniture designs. The use of a grid to make the project easy to complete at home was inspired by old school exercise books and the Tetris video game.

Ideas for furniture designs can be found in WEmake's Tetris inspiration leaflet – including this laid-back seat, an upright chair, dining table, bed, nest of tables, stool and magazine rack. Anyone can use the simple **10x10cm grid [2]** to create a template for their own unique designs. The making process begins with collecting some nice clean corrugated cardboard from the plentiful piles to be found around the back of most high streets, from supermarkets or in our own dustbins, and flattening it out.

After **marking out the profile [3]** of the Tetris design, a sharp craft knife or scissors are used to **cut out the shape [4]**. Orientation of the corrugated layers should be alternated to give structural strength. PVA glue

[5]

[6]

[7]

is ideal for **sticking the layers together [5]**.

This particular seat was made in six stacks, each taking around three hours to cut and glue, before being weighted down under a board and left to dry for a few hours or overnight. Finally all six sections were **stacked [6]** on top of each other and weighted down to dry. The whole seat was then coated with a couple of **protective layers of PVA [7]**.

There are endless ways to personalise Tetris: paint it, draw on it, apply stickers or decoupage decorations, or add re-used wallpaper, wrapping paper, or posters to the side panels. The finished piece is ideally designed for its maker to sit back and take a well-earned rest.

IN CONVERSATION WITH WEMAKE

What sparked the idea for this piece?
Discarded cardboard boxes, the video game, Frank Gehry, Blue Peter, old school exercise books.

What is the message behind your work?
Make It Yourself, go on - get creative! WEmake want you to get inspired and create your own designs from scrap.

Do you see this design developing further? If so, how?
WEmake hope Tetris will inspire people to play with cardboard and develop their own versions.

What are the environmental implications of your work?
Rubbish can be transformed, upgraded and given a new lease of life by anyone at their own kitchen table… WEmake better stuff, WEmake stuff better.

Does your work have an impact on a social level?
WEmake aim to demystify design and encourage creativity in others. We like to think we can make you smile too.

What made you start thinking about sustainability?
The gems that people decide to put in skips.

What makes a truly sustainable product?
Nature.

How can we turn manufacturers and specifiers on to sustainability?
Show them there is another, better way.

…and other designers?
See above.

Do you have any words of wisdom for new designers?
Use your power wisely.

Where do you get your best ideas?
Bed, bath, bus…

What motivates and inspires you?
Our daughter, the little Maker.

What was the last object you threw away?
Food packaging.

What was the last thing you fixed?
Probably the most recent thing that our little Maker 'unfixed'.

What is your guilty pleasure or biggest eco sin?
Driving.

If you could get everyone to do one thing every day, what would it be?
Make something better.

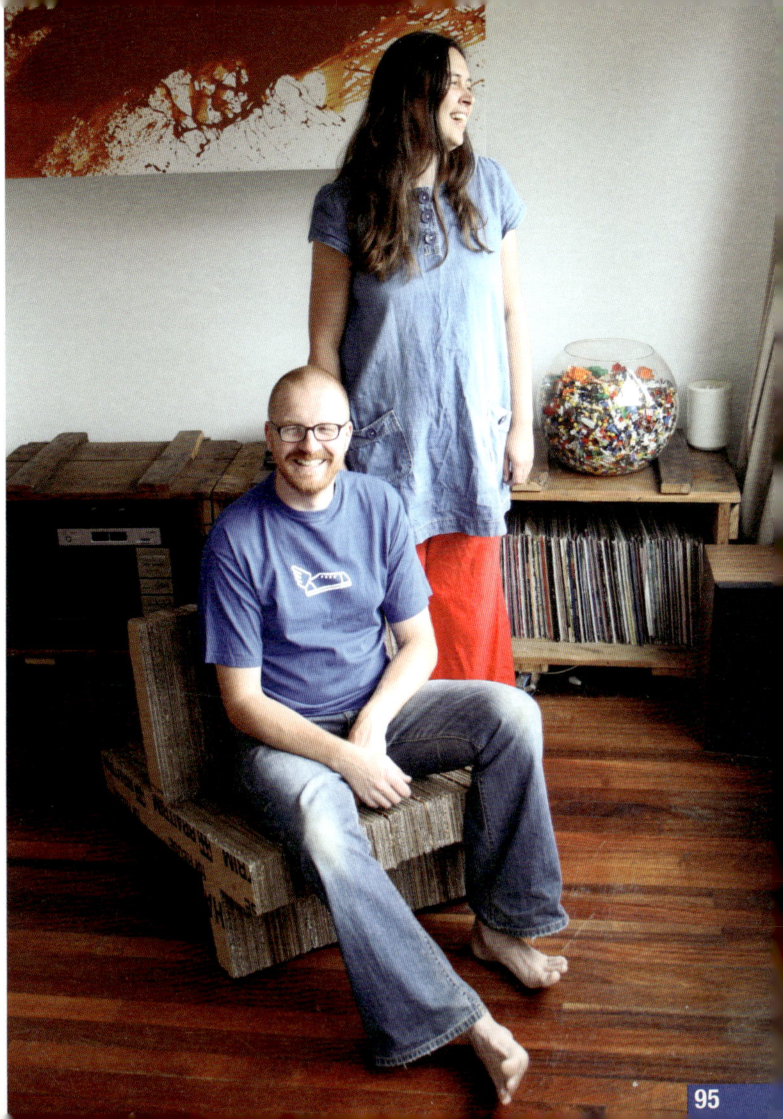

YOUR STOOL 2

RYUICHI TABU

A seat that transforms to suit its owner from childhood to old age: from a rocking horse, to a see-saw, to a full-backed rocking chair. Its multifunctional and customisabie design stimulates the user's imagination and creates an emotional bond with the product.

Dimensions: H 470mm x W 730mm x D 230mm

Materials: Plywood, wooden dowel rod

Tools: CNC, hand tools

[re]strategies: [re]source [re]spond

Back components fold down for different uses

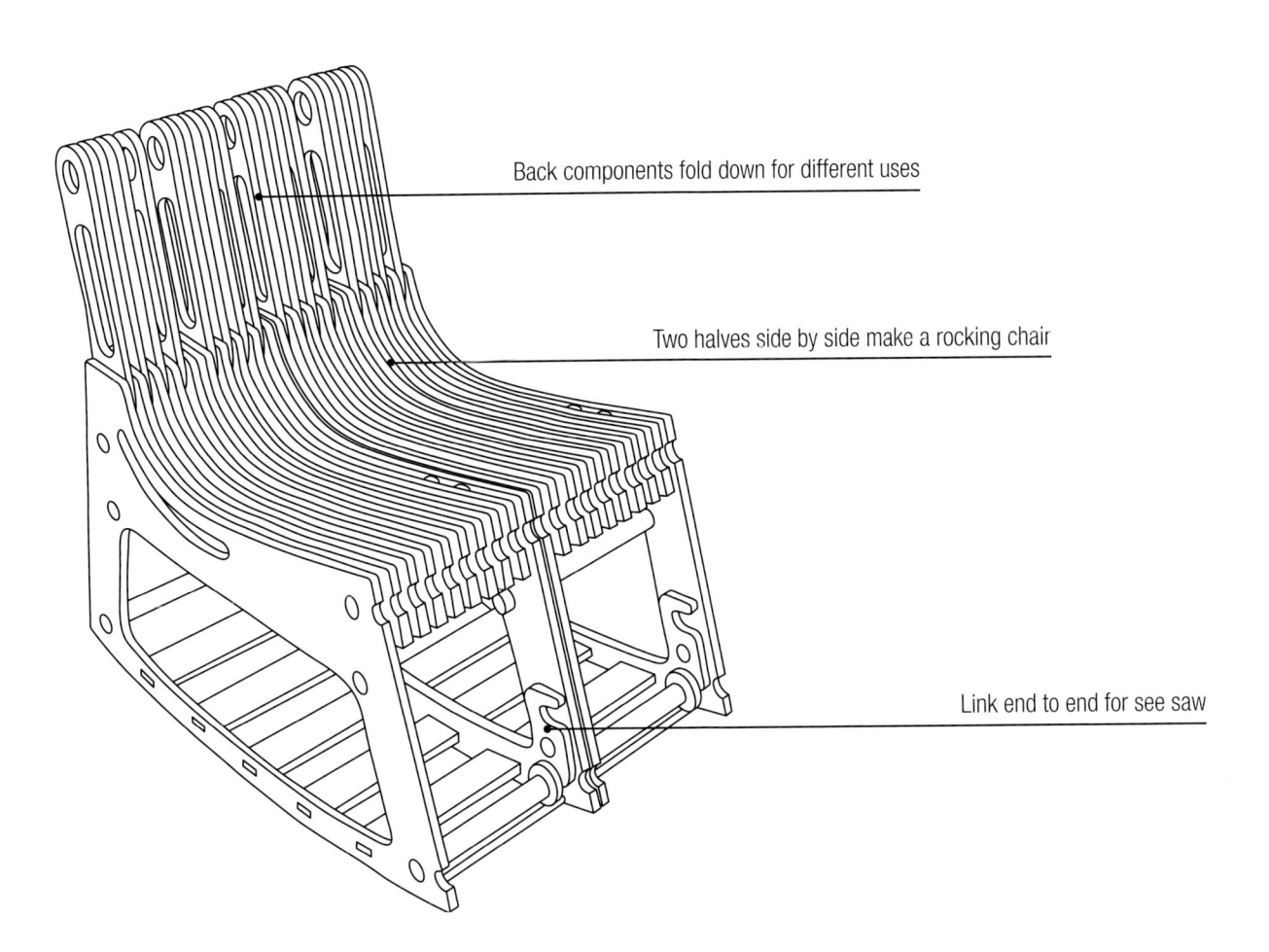

Two halves side by side make a rocking chair

Link end to end for see saw

THE MAKING OF YOUR STOOL 2

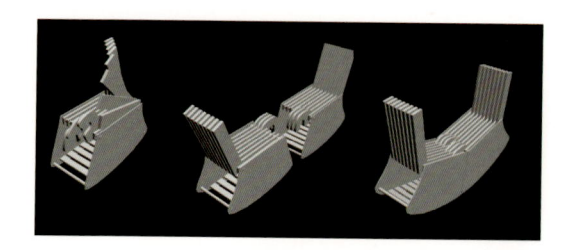

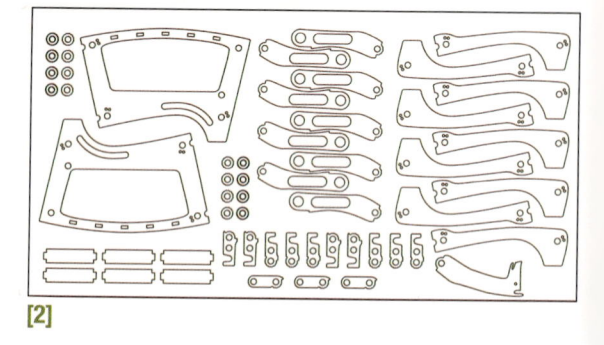

[1]

[2]

Your Stool 2 pioneers a new take on digital-bespoke production, developing a stronger creative connection between the designer, consumer and product. Its combination of a new aesthetic and efficient production addresses both ecological and human aspects of sustainability.

The design aims to challenge negative views of consumerism, instead enabling consumers to develop cultural identity through creative activity. A key idea is cultural sustainability, defined as "developing, renewing and maintaining human cultures that create long-term relationships with other people and the natural world".

According to designer Ryuichi Tabu, sustainability demands nothing less than "the symbiosis of culture, nature and economics". Your Stool 2 proposes a new product-service system based on the notion of **'well-beings' [1]** – considering the user's long-term enjoyment, creativity and quality of life. **New technologies and methods of production [2]** and distribution enable individual creative input, and complement more sustainable ways of living.

[3]

[4]

Through participating in an interactive online story, the consumer determines the final form of the product. The stool is manufactured digitally, with each component CNC cut from sustainably sourced plywood, using the designs created by the client's online input. The components are then **assembled by hand [3]**.

Your Stool 2 is designed to **stay with the user for a lifetime [4]**. Its multifunctionality stimulates the imagination and enhances emotional connection: it can take on a wide range of forms including a full-backed chair, a rocking horse or a see-saw. Through continuous interaction over time, the product becomes more of a companion than an object. Additional customisation is possible over the course of its lifetime, further enhancing this personal bond.

IN CONVERSATION WITH RYUICHI TABU

What sparked the idea for this piece?
Shel Silverstein's The Giving Tree.

What is the message behind your work?
A sense of fun and a deeper emotional attachment are just as important in allowing a product to be sustainable.

Do you see this design developing further? If so, how?
The form of the piece allows for further parts to be attached to create new customisation possibilities.

What are the environmental implications of your work?
Although it's important for materials and energy consumption to be sustainable, my primary focus as a designer is the sustainability of the product itself. In Shintoism, it is believed that all objects have souls and that is why Shintoists do not take the world around them for granted. By designing a work that has a "soul", or in this case a deep emotional bond with the user, I believe I have created a product that discourages the kind of waste associated with disposable, mass-produced items.

Does your work have an impact on a social level?
See above.

What made you start thinking about sustainability?
I am originally from Japan. Although it is a highly developed and industrialized country, as a society we are always conscious about the importance of preserving nature and not wasting resources such as water and electricity. Because I was brought up in such an environment, you could say I've been thinking about sustainability since I was born.

What makes a truly sustainable product?
I believe a truly sustainable product must be sustainable in both the physical sense and the metaphysical sense. The resources that go into it must be renewable, recyclable, etc., but the passion of the user that goes into the product itself must also be long-lasting and renewable.

How can we turn manufacturers and specifiers on to sustainability?
Manufacturers are neither good nor bad; if the product in question itself is sustainable, then the manufacturers of that product will be automatically working towards sustainability, and vice versa. So I believe this is more the responsibility of designers and consumers.

…and other designers?
Although I believe it would be a good idea to introduce the concept of sustainability to designers in schools, I think the emphasis should be that it is only one of many tools that a designer can use. Otherwise, designers may get the impression that all other design is somehow 'evil', which may discourage especially new designers from experimenting in any way.

Do you have any words of wisdom for new designers?
Not really. I'm still pretty new myself.

Where do you get your best ideas?
I don't get ideas, ideas come to me.

What motivates and inspires you?
Design, in all its various incarnations.

What was the last object you threw away?
Takeaway container.

What was the last thing you fixed?
My bicycle.

What is your guilty pleasure or biggest eco sin?
My nightlife (too much alcohol, greasy food).

If you could get everyone to do one thing every day, what would it be?
Play a musical instrument.

DESIGN YOUR OWN SEAT

SEAT:

DESIGNER:

Dimensions:

Materials:

Tools:

[re]strategies:

103

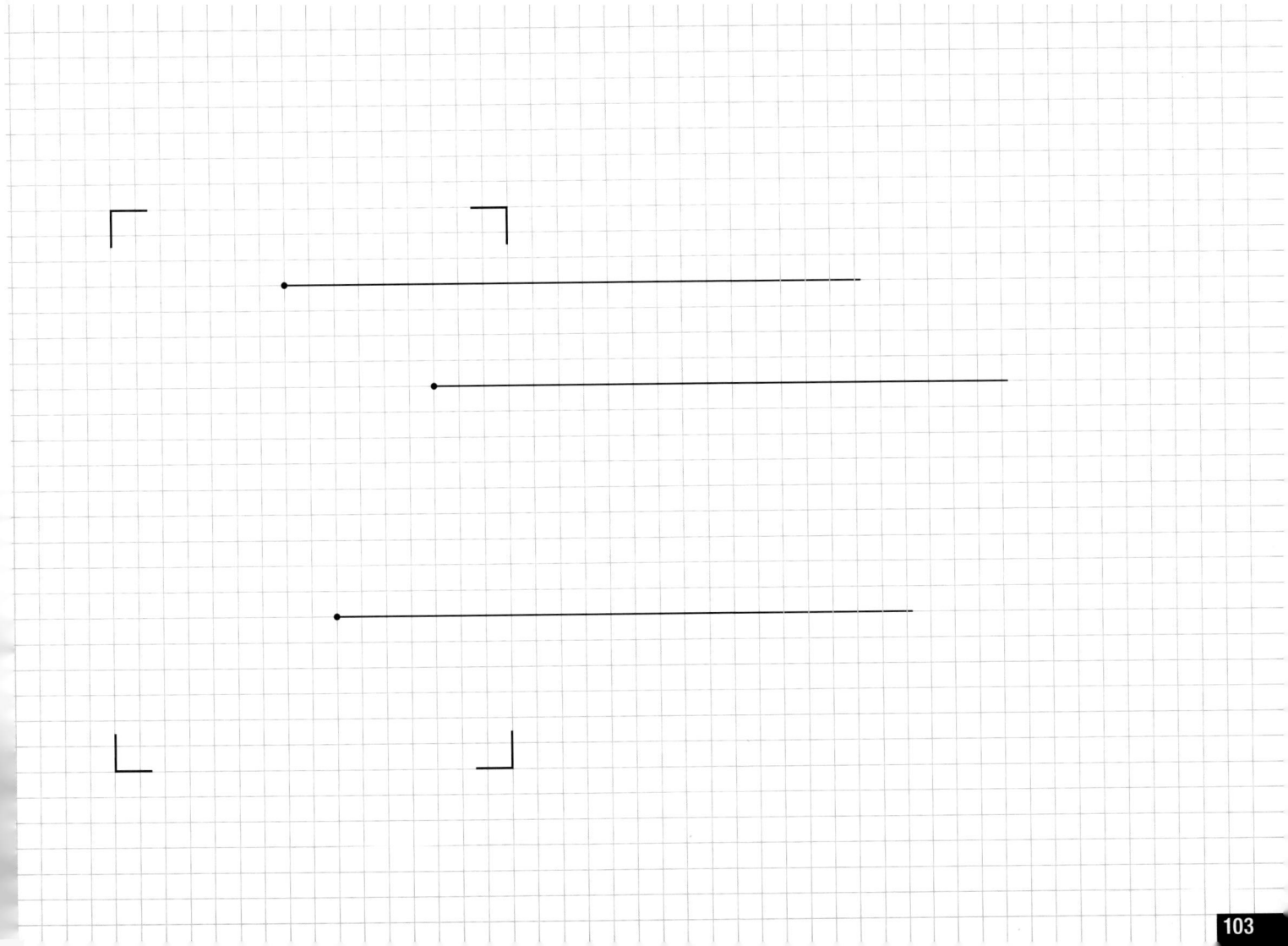

THE MAKING OF:

IN CONVERSATION WITH:

What sparked the idea for this piece?

What made you start thinking about sustainability?

What is the message behind your work?

What makes a truly sustainable product?

Do you see this design developing further? If so, how?

How can we turn manufacturers and specifiers on to sustainability?

What are the environmental implications of your work?

… and other designers?

Does your work have an impact on a social level?

Do you have any words of wisdom for new designers?

Where do you get your best ideas?

What motivates and inspires you?

What was the last object you threw away?

What was the last thing you fixed?

What is your guilty pleasure or biggest eco sin?

If you could get everyone to do one thing every day, what would it be?

[RE]DESIGN

[re]design is a not-for-profit organisation that supports the work of designers who don't want to make landfill. We are passionate about sustainable design and believe design can be a catalyst for positive social and environmental change.

[re]design seeks out and promotes products that are genuinely 'good' and gorgeous. We put together pioneering projects that spark and nurture sustainable design ideas, building relationships that help bring concepts to fruition.

Get in touch **www.redesigndesign.org**

[re]
DESIGN

likes you

[RE]STRATEGIES

[re]design have identified nine [re]strategies that are being used today to create design that's friendly to people and the environment.

[RE]CLAIM — Designs using waste materials in the raw, without reprocessing.

[RE]CREATE — Customised or personalisable designs – making an emotive connection between owner and object.

[RE]CYCLE — Designs made with reprocessed waste materials.

[RE]DUCE — Designs which minimise waste of energy and materials, are multifunctional, or raise awareness of resource use.

[RE]MAKE — Designs that allow easy, cost-effective disassembly and re-use of parts or recycling at end of life.

[RE]MIND — Characterful designs that evoke memories, reminding you to treasure them.

[RE]SOURCE — Designs using renewable natural materials, managed to ensure a sustainable supply.

[RE]SPOND — Sociable designs which invite interaction and friendliness.

[RE]USE — Designs making creative use of readymade, second-hand objects and components.

[RE]DESIGN GLOSSARY

Adaptable
Products that can change over time to meet users' needs.

Bespoke
Designs made to a user's specifications.

Biodegradable
Natural materials that can be broken down by living organisms and returned to the earth.

Built to last
Products made to last a lifetime.

Certified Organic
Materials that have been grown with minimal synthetic chemical intervention.

Clean manufacture
Production techniques avoiding unnecessary pollution.

Designed for disassembly
Designs that enable a product to be taken apart easily for recycling at end of life.

Designed for remanufacture
Products that can be refurbished or upgraded, by renovating and reassembling their components.

Designed for reuse
Products designed to have more than one lifetime, without requiring reprocessing of materials.

Dry joint construction
Products put together without the use of glues.

Efficient material use
Designs produced with minimal material wastage.

Energy efficient manufacture
Production techniques minimising the use of heat and electricity.

Enhanced by age
Products designed to develop character over time.

Evokes memories
Products made with materials that have a history and remind the user of good times.

Local materials
Materials produced locally to where the products are manufactured, saving energy in transport.

Measures resource use
Designs that monitor the use of resources such as electricity or water, raising awareness and encouraging efficiency.

Mend it yourself
Products that can be repaired by the user.

Mono-material
Products made from a single material, for easy recycling.

Multifunctional
Products that have more than one use.

Personalisable
Products designed for users to put their own mark on.

Reclaimed materials
Salvaged materials put to new uses without reprocessing.

Recyclable
Materials that can be reprocessed to be used again.

Renewably powered manufacture
Production powered by hand, by the sun, by wind…

Repairable
Products designed to be easily mended.

Reprocessed materials
New materials from old – discarded materials that have undergone industrial processing to make them usable again.

Reused parts
Discarded components or products that are incorporated whole into a new product, without being broken down into their constituent materials.

Self-make
Products designed to be made or assembled at home.

Sold locally
Products sold locally to where they are manufactured – saving energy in transport.

Sustainably grown materials
Natural materials grown in a way that maintains the long-term health of the environment they come from.

Take-back service
Products or parts that can be returned to the manufacturer at end of life for recycling.

Uses existing tooling
Designs that create new applications for existing tooling, moulds, jigs etc, avoiding the need to make new ones.

Water efficient manufacture
Production minimising the use of water (for cleaning, cooling etc).

IMAGE CREDITS

p 4-5
Courtesy Aaron Moore
Courtesy Ryan Frank
Courtesy David Colwell Design
Courtesy Alessandro Zampieri Design
Courtesy Christopher Cattle
Courtesy Blue Marmalade
Courtesy Orangebox
Courtesy Reestore
Courtesy Claire Heather-Danthois
Courtesy Lou Rota
Courtesy Cohda
© Pli Design
Courtesy Sam Murat
Courtesy Andrew Millar
Courtesy WEmake
Courtesy Ryuichi Tabu
p 6-11
Courtesy Aaron Moore
p 12-17
Courtesy Ryan Frank
p 18-23
Courtesy David Colwell Design
p 24-29
Courtesy Alessandro Zampieri Design
p 30-35
Courtesy Chris Cattle

p 36-41
Courtesy Blue Marmalade
p 42-47
Courtesy Orangebox
p 48-53
Courtesy Reestore
p 54-59
Courtesy Claire Heather-Danthois
p 60-65
Courtesy Lou Rota
p 66-71
Courtesy Cohda
p 72-77
© Pli Design/© Sprout Design
p 78-83
Courtesy Sam Murat
p 84-89
Courtesy Andrew Millar
p 90-95
Courtesy WEmake
p 96-101
Courtesy Ryuichi Tabu
p 102-107
Courtesy You